Revelation Now

Viewing the Tragedies and Triumph of Believers: Building Faith Now

A Commentary on the Book of Revelation

SHELLIE SAMPSON, JR

iUniverse, Inc.
New York   Bloomington

iUniverse books may be ordered through booksellers or by contacting:

iUniverse
1663 Liberty Drive
Bloomington, IN 47403
www.iuniverse.com
1-800-Authors (1-800-288-4677)

Because of the dynamic nature of the Internet, any Web addresses or links contained in this book may have changed since publication and may no longer be valid. The views expressed in this work are solely those of the author and do not necessarily reflect the views of the publisher, and the publisher hereby disclaims any responsibility for them.

ISBN: 978-1-4401-9747-5 (sc)
ISBN: 978-1-4401-9748-2 (ebook)
ISBN: 978-1-4401-9749-9 (dj)

Printed in the United States of America

iUniverse rev. date: 06/15/2010

Scripture quotations are taken from the King James version. Any other translations are the authors.

Contents

Preface

A Wider Perspective for a Better Life Now

In serving many disillusioned and hurting people in my pastoral assignment over many years, I am committed to a people-minded mission. In particular, my interest is in enabling people to live holistic, balanced lives in the situation they find themselves. An underlying theme in *Revelation Now* is how people handle their emotional responses to the difficulties they face In "anxiety society" (stressful environments). At the same time believers need a wider view on how to understand and interpret global society. The Prophet Hababkkuk states that the Lord answered me and said write the vision and make it plain... for the vision is yet for an appointed time...but the just shall live by faith. (2:2a, 3a, 4b)

People are living more and more in anxiety states, even though outwardly many appear to be "*normal*". It is our task, our felt responsibility, to help make a difference in how people are able to relate to the world. Uncertain times provide an occasion for persons to develop an overcoming faith.

My studying and teaching of the book of Revelation for many years has been reinforced through learning and travel. I have traveled to Rome and met with religious scholars there. I studied in Jerusalem as a part of a New York University learning tour as a graduate student. I traveled to Egypt and the great museum of history in Cairo as well as other parts of Africa. I am grateful for my studies in Hebrew, Greek, and church history at Drew University. I have a particular interest in human personality and the environment. I am currently involved with missions in Africa and urban challenges in the United States.

Introduction

What Is Going On? Earthquakes, Wars and Worry

Near the time of Jesus' departure the disciples were getting jittery. They were saying to him, "We need some answers." They were perplexed and almost frustrated. The disciples could see by the opposition and unbelief of some people that this mission was not going to be easy, and they were right. The disciples inquired of Jesus about end-time events and what were the signs of his return. In Matthew 24:3 their questions involved concerns about future conditions and happenings in a challenging and adversarial age.

Many scholars today are also concerned about these conditions. The times described in Matthew 24 also reflect present realities. They include the breakdown and rejection of traditional norms and universal respect for human life. During these postmodern times, the social-political state of nations and the natural environment reflect an increase in the irregular patterns of turmoil. Relationships suffer more because insecure people retreat into defensive tendencies, excessive self-love (narcissism), and mistrust. Global society tends to become more stratified in terms of increased competition, divided loyalties and extreme economic disparities.

In difficult times we must watch, pray, and carefully plan our lives. Those who try to operate without critical reflection will become candidates for added stress, manipulation, and deception. Some aspects of these conditions are discussed in 2 Timothy 3:1–4, 13. A firm point of reference will be needed for devalued, unfocused, marginalized people. Spiritual inspiration is needed for personal comfort and clear perceptions in a troubled world of restricted freedoms.

Deuteronomy 29:29 reminds us that God is a revealing God ("The secret things belong unto the LORD our God: but those things which are revealed belong unto us and to our children for ever, that we may do all the words of this law.") Secrets are unfolded and revealed by him. God does not want us to be uninformed, unprepared, and without a faith direction during times of woe and crisis. He acts as a revealer of mysteries and an enabler of people. In the book of Revelation, God acts to unfold the coming events for waiting believers who live in "the challenging now." Remember, end-times do not come at one time but in stages. There are hidden, connected events that lie before our eyes. As the vultures focus upon the bodies of the failing, so shall critical events become more obvious to those who focus upon them (Matthew 24:28). The challenges of current difficult times motivate believers and nonbelievers to think about prime movers, makers, and shapers in the world whose actions affect many people.

In the days of Noah, people were preoccupied with day-to-day activities despite prophetic warning. They were spiritually unfocused and inattentive right until the very end. So it is today. There will be many strange happenings, but we are not to jump to conclusions. Events and global trends are subject to much reflection and interpretation. Current trends and shifts seem to be moving in some kind of global direction. But the end is not yet (Matthew 24:6). According to Matthew 24:33 they are at the door. We should not become careless, anxious, or complacent. We should not become unjust and merciless ourselves. We should not engage in vindictive actions because of our difference. We should not think that we will not be affected by world events. In fact, throughout the Bible God's people were affected by contextual powers and international politics. It is not for us to fix dates on history but to respond to reality. The purpose of this book is not to review all the major interpretations or details about the setting and composition of Revelation, but to pay close attention to the important features of Revelation that speak to our lives now.

Revelation Now is not about looking at life in a gloomy way. It is not about making doomsday predictions. It is about the plain awareness of how life is ever-changing and that we should have hope and assurance beyond circumstances. Believers must always believe! When the Son of man returns, he will be looking for faith on the earth. (Luke 18:8) The point is to relate to an ever-present God no matter what. By faith we can navigate a better life despite disadvantages, hardships, and economic collapse. As we learn more about the book of Revelation, we will also learn to live under more pressing conditions, when necessary.

The Historic Patmos Setting: Blamed, Banned, and Blessed

Believers need to read the Bible often, especially the New Testament, and rejoice in the revealing messages written by inspired saints. But there is more to the story. There is a whole lot going on in between the lines and the twenty-seven New Testament books. The Roman Empire was present as a hostile stronghold of unbelief. The terrain for creating faith in people was difficult and challenging. It took a lot of spiritual courage to deal with the forces of power, greed, and opposition. Most of the targeted population present on the missionary agenda of Jesus, Paul, and John had not even heard of the Holy Spirit, faith, resurrection, or a world to come.

The book of Revelation was written during the time of a dominating military, political, and economic empire. In fact, most of the Bible was written under similar conditions. People sometimes gain deeper insights during periods of great challenge. The Gospels, the Epistles, and the Hebrew Bible were all written in the context and background of some dominating world power. Discussions of faith, salvation, liberation, and the Kingdom of God were oppositional and subversive in nature. Christian writers, however, encouraged believers to honor lawful requirements and be good citizens. At the same time a life of faith was encouraged for all believers.

The Roman world was very much present in New Testament references. Historic rulers and personalities mentioned include Cyrenius, Pontius Pilate, Herod, Agrippa, Caesar Augustus, and the centurion. The high priests were either appointed or approved by the local Roman ruler. Biblical writings went beyond narrow Judaistic issues and religious disputes. In a more subtle way, the writings created a forum to engage a larger realm of life. This life included the cultural world of Rome, pagan gods, customs, emperor worship, and

Greek-Roman philosophy. The impact of Stoic and Gnostic beliefs are hidden in Pauline writings and the book of Acts.

The last book of the Christian Bible includes many references to the Hebrew Bible and its historical context as well. There is a continuity of history between the two testaments. John lived in the context of the Roman Empire which was a continuation of a string of empires that helped influence many of the background events present from Abraham to Moses and from Jesus and Paul to finally John on the Isle of Patmos. In fact, many of the symbols and images John uses refer to the many nations mentioned in the Hebrew Bible. The context of the Hebrew Bible includes powers from Egypt/Kush (Ethiopia), Assyria, Babylon, Persia, Greece, and Rome.

The author who called himself John was located (in exile) on the Island of Patmos, which was five by ten miles long. Patmos was in the sea lane between Ephesus and Rome.

John's revelation is introduced through messages to seven churches located in seven city-states in Asia Minor (now Turkey). All these cities had some political, cultural, and economic ties to Rome. These ties also included prevalent practices related to emperor worship, materialism, imperial cults, and contrasting philosophical beliefs (Colossians 2:8). There was also present in the culture certain social inequalities (James 2:2–6; 1 Corinthians 8:4–5) classism, sexism, and immoral pagan practices (1 Corinthians 14:33; Ephesians 4:19).

The perspective of New Testament readers went beyond parochial religious concerns to the spiritual condition and lifestyle of an entire empire. In fact, the integrity and authority of the new Christian faith was seen in contrast to the corrupt pagan world. The New Testament is set in the middle of an ungodly world order and decadent global society. It is concerned about legitimate witness, just governance, global righteousness, human oppression, and the need for universal repentance before God (Revelation 2:19). The focus is upon the kingdom of this world versus the Kingdom of our Lord. "And the seventh angel sounded; and there were great voices in heaven, saying, The kingdoms of this world are become the kingdoms of our Lord, and of his Christ; and he shall reign for ever and ever" (Revelation 11:15). The role of this biblical Jesus expands from the messianic fulfillment of "the one who is to come" to the global Christ who returns to reign as the Lord of Lords and King of Kings. "How great are his signs! and how mighty are his wonders! his kingdom is an everlasting kingdom, and his dominion is from generation to generation" (Daniel 4:3). "The field is the world; the good seed are the children of the kingdom; but the tares are the children of the wicked one" (Matthew 13:38). "Jesus answered, My kingdom is not of this world: if my kingdom were of this world, then would my servants fight, that I should not be delivered to the Jews: but now is my kingdom not from hence" (John 18:36).

The one who is first and last in Revelation 1:11, speaks to those who are in time and place (*temporal* beings). He gives his audience a bigger picture, a wider view of the collective human experience in the world. He moves beyond the scenes to provide a sense of divine providence, clarity, and meaning. There is more to be understood beyond the actual events themselves. All events are related.

The Secure Love of God

Some readers may ask, does God fall out of love? Why would God allow those he is supposed to love to suffer? Even those who live godly lives will suffer. (2 Timothy 3:12; 1 Corinthians 4:12; 2 Corinthians 4:8–9)

God has never ceased to love his creatures and his creation. It is because of his divine, benevolent character that we are even here. God's love is present in every trial. His love is *Hesed*, steadfast love (Hebrew). It reflects the self-imposed generosity of God toward all of us. Jesus himself endured a suffering love (*agape*, Greek) for us as well.

However, the process of events concerning good and evil must run its course. God permits the expressions of different persuasions to exalt his own ultimate cause. The contrast between good and evil is clearly seen. And through everything that happens God's love can be seen. It is also available to all. God desires love, repentance, and faith in response to his grace. He defeats evil for our liberation and life. He is the life giver. He protects our long-range interest and ultimate deliverance. The evil order does not want to submit or be regulated in any manner. But there is every reason to believe the living Lord and trust his Word even as we experience affliction. Too many take God for granted and take his offer of grace lightly (Matthew 22:1–5).

But the conditions of a defiant, problematic global society bring our need for God back to our reality.

> And Jesus answered and spake unto them again by parables, and said, The kingdom of heaven is like unto a certain king, which made a marriage for his son, And sent forth his servants to call them that were bidden to the wedding: and they would not come. (Matthew 22:1–3)

In the book of Revelation, the struggle moves beyond groups of individuals to mega powers and principalities. The challenged believer has nothing to fear when he or she submits to the love and compassion of a redeemer God-king — **The Alpha and Omega**. This title First and Last is unique to this book.

The Alpha and Omega in a Postmodern Age

The postmodern age is characterized as one in which there are no canons (set principles and practices). Everything is open to scrutiny, reinterpretation, and redefining. There are no fixed rules. Specialty groups, such as feminists, capitalists, and law enforcement agencies create their own canons, ways of thinking, and operating assumptions. From teaching to torture, from silence to violence, preferred practices become doctrine. Rules are often made to accommodate a context or group interest. The use of a defining rationale brings about added control and influence when introduced to a perplexed group. Past social and constitutional norms fade under specific conditions. Rulers select those practices and norms that justify their ideas and social position.

Culture, political orientation, and ethnicity can inform belief practices. But they may not reflect the eternal wisdom of the Alpha and Omega, Christ is all encompassing. Postmodernism challenges all religions, including Christianity, to demonstrate authenticity. The reality of Christ should become "visible" to a doubting world. The fruits of faith must be evident to the world. Postmodernism represents a great opportunity to affirm the clear wisdom of God and the Lordship of Christ. It is more profitable to move beyond doctrine and organized religion to a more powerful living witness.

The world is in constant motion. Every aspect of human life is affected such as: global politics, communications, economic systems, weather patterns, and human conflict. The nature of human power relationships (local and global) are constantly shifting too. This includes the shifting of practices and policies to adjust market conditions of world resources such as oil, water, and greenery. Greenery refers to forestry, agriculture, and valuable flora. The world state of human health, wealth, and religious conflict is impacting billions of lives. Yet, everything that happens is grounded in an emerging past that becomes visible in the moving present. All of life is connected and contiguous, a part of a whole. Most events operate within a cause-and-effect continuum. The book of Revelation has many hidden connected elements that are at the same time right in front of us. The magnitude of principalities and powers are unfolding before us on a grand scale.

We need to know about the forces, influences, and events that surround us. People need to know how the world is organized around them and how to recognize impacting powers and influences that in the past were unnoticed. This is important for developing decision-making skill and insight.

One of the best ways to examine where we are in the world is to revisit history. There are different ways of looking at the world beyond media presentation. You can look at the world from a historic point of view and follow the time line of human events. You can follow the lives of influential persons. You can examine the use of science and technology in nations. You can even look at the effects of genetic engineering, war, climate changes, geopolitics, world economics, materialism, and culture and human organizations. Topics such as governance, urban societies, religion, and language study also help us gain insight. These topics can show a great deal about human world trends and population shifts and how each affects the course of history.

I have chosen to examine the biblical record in light of current trends to better understand where the world seems to be going now. History is gradual and interconnected. Events in the past and future have continuity. I also see a relationship between all of the topics just mentioned with what the Bible says about humans in general. In fact, all events and sources of knowledge are related one way or another. For example, trying events have a psychological effect on people who are living through these happenings. The world itself is a psychological field with significant players. What is happening in your neighborhood and in your family is a consequence of unnoticed influences. These forces, policies, and ideologies (viewpoints) affect all of us. These influences help inform how we think, reason, and behave. We interact within the global context. The scripture reveals kernels of insights that relate to human thinking and emotion. It is a book about human behavior and the increasing effect of structured good and evil. It is about competing kingdoms of this world. At the same time, the loving outreach of God is projected through scripture. God has already shown his love in deliverance, forgiveness, and answered prayers. He brings us mental and emotional peace as we enter into his "rest." At the same time we can be confident in him who has brought us into his "rest" or spiritual well-being (Hebrews 4:3)

The book of Revelation offers a framework with which we are able to work out some kind of perspective on world events. It is not a detailed account of everything that occurs in life, but it helps us understand a bigger picture of the current states of affairs. Information from many parts of the Bible contributes to this picture. We are in this picture somewhere as we seek to make sense out of the world.

The writer of Revelation no doubt believed that God wanted us to be aware of the foes, woes, and conditions that war against us. This does not mean we should be obsessed with negative world events, but it does mean we can plan and pray over our lives in a more specific manner. God wants you to know the adversarial nature of the world. You don't have to stop living and pursuing the blessed life. At the same time, don't be ignorant of the times and the seasons that affect your daily existence.

Observing also means that we can begin to see better the kind of leadership, faith, and discipline that we are going to need in a radically changing world. This world will increasingly challenge our ability to maintain a high level of personal faith and group spirituality. Believers and would-be believers need some sense of warning and preparation for a life of overwhelming events and adversities. There is less benefit in talking about a crisis or a flood after the fact. "A word spoken in due season, how good is it!" (Proverbs 15:23).

Believers are going to have to dig a little deeper in developing a theology (a set of related spiritual beliefs and ideas) that can help in understanding the world as it is developing now. Theology uses biblical insights to inform and empower believers to endure and to make a difference. Saints can rise above and live through adversity. Hard conditions and the struggle to survive are going to become a way of life for more and more people. This challenge is not confined to the great tribulation, but a tribulation of ongoing hardness. "Principalities and powers" that seem to run the world order on every level seek to develop a master plan for global human life (Ephesians 6:12). Marginalized groups and isolated individuals in particular stand to suffer the most from end-time conditions. People need people. People need God. People need to increase their faith in God.

Some of these conditions are obvious; others are disguised. All are challenging. "Yea, and all that will live godly in Christ Jesus shall suffer persecution" (2 Timothy 3:12). The ungodly will suffer more. The way of the transgressor is hard! How shall we escape if we neglect so great a salvation? It is during this era that salvation will have greater meaning. It will provide more comfort and assurance than anything else on earth (1 John 5:4). Jesus said we need to search the scripture and know the power of God. "Search the scriptures; for in them ye think ye have eternal life: and they are they which testify of me" (John 5:39.) "And Jesus answering said unto them, Do ye not therefore err, because ye know not the scriptures, neither the power of God?" (Mark 12:24). Even before the great tribulation, there are hints of growing challenges and hardship for those who live in a world that is by definition evil. To be in the world at all includes some suffering.

The Structure of the Revelation

The book of Revelation has several forms intervening at the same time. It has many messages and layers of content. The content includes prophecy, hidden or disclosed information about the future. The future, however, is both now and later. It is generally agreed that the book was written under the selective oppression of Rome and its emperor Domitian about AD 96. The writer, John, wrote while under exile on the Isle of Patmos. Scholars believe John wrote the book over a period of time, not in one sitting. The person called John may or may not be the same John who wrote the gospel of John according to some scholars. Others believe that this is the same John who authored the forth gospel. This John was apparently sent into exile because of his uncompromising proclamation about Jesus as the divine Christ. John witnessed and testified of his persuasions in the context of other religious sects, and patron gods. It was probably his agitation of these groups that provoked his exile. Under conditions of exile, isolation and personal retreat John engages in an apocalyptic vision. Like Ezekiel and other post exilic prophets, John looks at the larger picture of cosmic conflict and the coming end of history. Revelation has parallel meaning both for the original historic setting and for conditions present in today's world. Prophesies and pronouncements speak to more than one generation. The ultimate meaning and application of the book unfolds gradually. Sometimes our present conditions provoke our need to seek ultimate vision.

The book is a letter that was to be circulated and read among the churches in the province of Asia Minor. It was to be narrated for the audience to hear and interpret its contextual message and future outlook. The letter has a message of evaluation, self-examination, warning, and expected challenges. It is a letter of consciousness raising and reflection. It is especially relevant to servant believers who already have a transcendent way of looking at the world. These servants already possess a certain level of knowledge and awareness about the biblical world, good and evil. The book points to the redemptive acts of God in bringing about a triumphant humanity. Revelation is seen as both a wakeup call and an expression of divine love. Love is kind enough to warn, to share truth, and work for the best victorious outcome.

The book provides a framework to view connecting apocalyptic (end-time) insight from the Old Testament and New Testament books as well as contemporary life and history. Different parts of the Bible provide certain information that can help fill in the general apocalyptic framework. Sayings from Daniel, Jesus, Paul, and others have a place in this framework. That does not mean we can precisely connect every event or idea related to the apocalypse. No one can. However, we can attempt to make sense out of what is available to us and relates to our lives now. These points are extremely important for those who question the inclusion of the book of Revelation in the New Testament canon. The book is not foreign or incompatible with other biblical texts. Some writers feel that the book is out of sync with the rest of the Bible. This is because of its inclusion of so much turbulence and less apparent use of theological terms like grace, mercy, and compassion. The purpose of any book is reflected in its use of language. This book deals with empire conditions. The book is also criticized because it seems to encourage people who advocate an Armageddon war and who want the world to end soon. But the agenda of those who desire an early war/clash and the motives for writing the book of Revelation may be entirely different. Our thoughts and ways may not be the thoughts of God and the best that God wants for us in the world at any given time. The story is not over yet. "And he said unto them, It is not for you to know the times or the seasons, which the Father has put into his own power." (Acts 1:7)

The Revelation framework includes a spiral of repeated ideas, themes, and concepts. A spiral is a circular, spring-like ring of ideas that develop from the past into the future. Ideas such as the lamb, evil, repentance, the Kingdom, death, the Messiah, and worship are included. These ideas or descriptions were introduced in the ancient world and continue today with expanded complexities in the historic context. The stakes get higher as variations in these end-time manifestations impact global life now. Our understanding of the past and future trends becomes clearer as the events of history unfold. We now have more tools and information to work with. We can see life as a larger spectrum of critical connecting episodes. Sometimes these events overlap as they develop. They are repeated in different ways. Our desire is to make sense out of what can appear as sporadic actions occurring without reason, purpose, connection, and direction. In fact, events in the world require some interpretation for meaning and survival. People need to ask, "What forces and systems are at work moving the world in the direction it appears to be going?"

There is also a theological perspective or framework that holds Revelation together. John had a particular theological worldview. His views define the purpose, content, and contributing ideas from a specific position of faith. In other words, the writer already had an experience of faith and a personal view of Christology (the love, life, and role of Christ). The writer was obviously familiar with the Hebrew world, one sovereign God, the twelve tribes of Israel, and the temple of God, for example. Hebrew concepts, symbols, angels, prophets, and related places like Babylon, Egypt, and the Euphrates River are also included in the imagery of the book. These images and terms come out of a Hebrew context.

At the same time, the political context of the Roman world and its meaning for future empires and people is also present. Use of the seven churches, angels, seals, trumpets, bowls, dragon, beast, harlot, Satan, the Lamb, Armageddon, and Babylon all blend together to present a great salvific drama through an overcoming Christ. The writer sees a connection of these intertwined ideas with human history. The particulars do not obscure the larger meaningful picture. Symbols are powerful expressions of a perceived reality.

Seven as an Organizing Principle of Concepts and Events

Seven represents a prominent number in the book of Revelation. It is used to organize and frame the entire book. There are many other symbols and concepts in the book, but all of them fit into the whole of a theological perspective (Ephesians 2:20–21).

This number is not new to scripture. It is a number of completion, perfection, and wholeness. Most of all it represents total fulfillment. Christ is the fulfillment of messianic prophecy, ministry, and redemption. A completed Christology of dominion and reign is seen in the book.

Some of the scriptural references of seven in nature and events include:

Seven days in the week of creation (Genesis 2:1–3)
Seven years of plenty and seven years of famine in Egypt (Genesis 41:28–31)
Seven times blood is to be sprinkled upon the altar of the Lord in the sanctuary (Leviticus 4:17–18)
Seven priests, horns, marches, and soundings (Joshua 6:8–9)

Seven things that God hates (Proverbs 6:16)

Seven times the just shall be redeemed (Proverbs 24:16)

Seven lamps and seven connections on one lamp and bowl (Zechariah 4:2)

Seven churches, angels, bowls (seven last plagues) eyes, heads, lamps, messengers, spirits, stars, trumpets, seals, thunders, etc. (the entire book of Revelation)

Seven demons (Luke 11:26)

Seven dips in the water (2 Kings 5:10, 14)

Seven sneezes (2 Kings 4:35)

Seven years of tribulation as the seventieth week of Daniel 9:27 (Matthew 24:15, 21)

Seven praises per day (Psalm 119:164)

Seven loaves of bread (Mark 8:5)

Seven social classes as the total social order or stratification (Revelation 6:15): kings (rulers), great persons (major public figures), rich (upper class, affluent), chief captains (military officers, law officers, institutional and religious heads), mighty men/women, (politicians, middle managers), slaves (lower working class, the working poor), free persons (ordinary, law-abiding citizens)

The number seven relates to the total accountability of the churches and believers. The warfare with evil, the wrath against the wicked, the seven major background nations of the Bible, and the seven new things to come (heaven, earth, city, nations, river, tree, and throne)are important to the complete picture.

John felt the urge and necessity to share his end-time views and experiences. Because he did share, we can make sense out of the sacrifices of martyrs who held to their faith, awaiting the vengeance and vindication of God himself. Exercising faith in God is in itself an act of resistance to other forces in the world. Christ has given saints a view of an unshakable kingdom with rights and power. Partnership in this kingdom defies and eventually overcomes the kingdom of darkness. The saints now move from suffering servants into reigning authority through the absolute sovereignty of Christ. Many themes and events can be observed through time and history as global rulers begin to execute policies that will affect the world population.

Conceptual Spiral Themes:
The Puzzle of Faith and Reality

In the history of faith there are many concepts at work as factors in the dramatic contest of good and evil. This chart reflects the combination of many factors that we must contend with. They arise from real life, Old and New Testament history. These factors are moving circular themes that weave around and forward toward eventual resolution. They occur over and over again, seen and unseen in the history of faith. As these factors, concepts, and ideas manifest themselves at various stages in human history as real events, the contemporary reader can point them out. These observations can become personal lessons for self and group management. People can learn from history and improve on the quality of their lives in the process of study. Faith grows under challenge if applied. You must look at each part of the puzzle and connect these ideas.

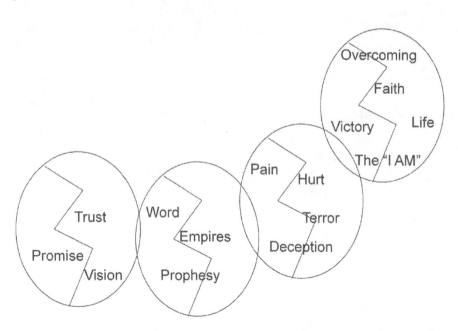

The Reality of Faith and Struggle

(From the Old Testament up to the New)
Life in the World Now

Reaching the Lost: The Focus: Revelation 1:5
              The Exalted Christis: 1:8
              End-time Preparation: Jude 20-25
              The Defeated devil: 1:18

The Responsibility of Faith: Watchful, faithful, prayerful, wisdom-filled, faith-management, steadfast performance (Matthew 24:42-45; Mark 13:33)

The Struggle for well-being: *Revelation Now*
When I would do good evil is always present: Romans 7:7-9, 11, 15

Two Domains of Negative Influence
Cosmic and Personal

1) Devil promotes terror, fear, unbelief—divide and conquer on a global society level
2) There are stages of anxiety, panic attacks, depressive, resentment, insecurity

God warns and promotes salvation, faith, and gospel truth—wholeness in peace, rest, or challenge

The spirit presence and the assurance of *"the Word"* and the Gospel of Christ renews hope and faith

Aim: Repentance, Revival, Resurrection, Reunion
Agents: Evil, unclean spirits verses the Holy Spirit

Old Testament, Influences in Revelation

275 or more Old Testament references and inferences in the 404 verses in the book

Symbols — Events — Themes
Old Testament: Prophecy and Struggle: Genesis 3:1, 4-5;
Joshua 24:15

Daniel Dreams about: 70 weeks of Exile, Empires, Rulers, Angels, Israel, people of God. Ezekiel envisions: an ox, man, eagle, lion, twelve tribes, evil spirits, Gog, Gomer Note: Isaiah sees the Messiah (Chapters 9 and 11) within a temple-centered theocracy (Chapter 6).

Messianic appearance is envisioned in the Book.

Zechariah sees Angels, 2 olive trees, horses, Jerusalem, truth, final conflict, Valley of Megiddon, false prophets, plague, God's kingdom, worship in his visions and prophesies.

The Fall, The Law vs the Lawless Ones Daniel 7:25 (to be later explained) Genesis, Exodus, The Word Unfolds God's deliverance.

Deliverance (Exodus) Sin, Rejection, the Altar, Living Sacrifice (Genesis) rebellion, disobedience, murder, Serpent, subtle seduction, Paradise, Promise Land anticipated Oppression.

New Testament Continuity: Hidden Empire and Kingdom Themes

(John reports (3:3, 3:31, 19:19; 21) that the Christological Kingdom does exist. References to an ongoing kingdom imply a rival domain that transcends earthly empires. This is also seen in light of the prayer "let the kingdom come." This Kingdom excels in significance and power. It is about life and not death. "...Jesus came into Galilee preaching the gospel of the kingdom of God and saying the time is fulfilled and the kingdom of God is at hand..." Mark 1:14. Paul used his Roman citizenship to negotiate his cosmic Christian faith and his personal justification before Caesar. "Then said Paul, I stand at Caesar's judgment seat, where I ought to be judged: to the Jews have I done no wrong, as thou very well knowest. I appeal unto Caesar. Then Festus, when he had conferred with the council, answered, Hast thou appealed unto Caesar? unto Caesar shalt thou go" (Acts 25:10–12). Here we have two world views and kingdoms confronting each other in the same context.

Major Powers: Empires Now

Modern Empires
Russia, China, Europe, USA (Islamic Nations sometimes included as a possible religious empire)
Post-industrial, postmodern period of mega structures
Micromanaged society, overlapping administration of many institutions
Technological communication network, global culture and ideology
Modern global cities—centers of influence and specialties
"Habitus"—globalized thinking/minds (collective social influence)

Historic Background, Biblical Narratives include an ongoing empire presence in the backgrounds
Divided Kingdom, exile into empire territories
collective beastly symbols
The Prophets, refer to Egypt, Ethiopia, Babylon, Assyria, Persia, Greece, Rome
David 1,000 BCE (Messianic king type)
The lure of idolatry, syncretism, and foreign culture (II Samuel to II Chronicles)
People and empires are connected through geneology (genetics), gemometry, and proto-language in pre-history
(basic roots of a generalized language which becomes more specific as development occurs)

Postmodern Global Clashes/Conflict

Empires: international influence, new emerging empires, and economics

Religions: dominant beliefs and practices are in tension major religions have major influence and agendas

Classes: extreme disparities/inequalities (social stratification) in the world order

The Spiral of Unfolding History

Themes: Old and New Testament Anticipates the New Order

End-Time Realities

Overcoming Faith and Overcoming Life (1 John 5:4-5)
The Resurrection of the Dead
New Babylon
The New Creation, Revelation 13, 21
The Dragon, Beast, and False Prophets
Misinformation, Deception
The Seven Seals, Revelation 6
Daniel 7:25
End-Times

Religion as Practiced in time

Regions such as Assyria, Babylon, Ethiopia, Egypt, Persia, Greece, and Rome.
Eastern or Western civilization as the model image of true humanity, and the theocratic Current players/Islamic world, Buddhism, Hinduism, Science, Humanist society, Secular Society (Where there is no need or desire for God)

Religion by Past Traditions

Complexity of Life, Jude 1:6
2 Peter 2, 2 Timothy 3
Hebrews 7:19–26
Worldwide Ministry—Outreach,
Acts 17:16-34
Disciples, Gifts of the Spirit

Postmodern Global Society Institutionalized Structures

International bodies, alliances, world economy
Massive Evil, god as money, power, control
Structured Evil, Blasphemy, World government

New Kingdom Arrivals

The Resurrected Christ Enthroned

New Testament Clash of Belief Systems and civilizations

Control of the use of Time and affect human life. God's universal concern: God's love no respecter of persons (Acts 10:34)

Leaders who Confront Empire Exodus 14:4; 19:46, Acts 25:1-5

The Second Coming: the Messianic King

Paradise: Heaven Regained

Cosmic Calamities, Kingdom Conflicts, Global Wars, disputes

The New Witness, the Spirit Poured Out

The Temple Destroyed, No More Animal Sacrifices (AD 70)

Worldwide Ministry—Hebrews 8:6 Witnesses

The Church versus Hegemony: Glorious Worship, New Jerusalem

The Great Judgment: The King, The Lamb, the Judge

Apocalypse Events, Issues and Anti-Christ Spirit

Revelation	Other	Antichrist, Wicked One Lawless one
Non-Peace	6:4	Chief rebel) man of Sin/son of
Economics	6:6	perdition, Agent of self-exaultation
Mass Murder	6:8	messianic imitation, opposition
Hunger	6:9	1 John 2:18, 4:3, 2 Thessalonia 2:3, 18
Earthquakes	6:12; 16–18	Matthew 24:7
Hatred		Matthew 24:9 John 15:18–19
Second Coming	1:7	Matthew 24:30; 1 Corinthians 15:24
Kingdom of Priests	1:6; 5:10	1 Peter 2:9

Tribulation	2:10; 3:10; 7:14; 11:2	Matthew 24:21, 29
Worship	4:10–11, 5:13–14	
The Kingdom	11:15, 12:10	
Plagues	9:20; 15:6	
Performance	2:19; 3:15	
Repentance		
Fornication: Idolatry	17:2l, 4l; 18:3; 3:21	
Witness	11:3	
Torture/Terror	9:5; 11:13	
Allegiance	17:12–13	
Word Response	11:10	
Institutions/Structures		
Ecosystems	12:3; 13:1–4;	
	17:1–10; 15-18;	Ephesians 6:12
Prayer	8:3	
Disease	16:2	
Relationships	2:4; 2:20; 3:17;	
	6:11; 12:4; 21:8	Matthew 24:10–12;
		Mark 13:2;
		John 15:19
Demon Power	16:13–14; 14:19–20;	
	13:4, 12, 15	
War Machines	9:3, 7	
Faith/Patience	13:10; 14:12; 2:13, 19	Luke 18:8
God's Power	15:8; 16:9	
Final Victory/Judgment	20:1–3, 21:6; 22:7;	
	19:20	1 Corinthians 15:24–28;
		1 Thessalonians 4:13–18;
Betrayals/Mistrust	18:4; 2:20; 3:9	Mark 13:12;
		Matthew 24:10, 12;
		Matthew 10:21-22, 34-40;
		2 Timothy 3:13
Fires	8:7; 9:18; 16:8	
Volcanoes	8:8	
Ships Sinking	8:9	

Water Pollution	8:11	
Armageddon	16:16	
Prophecy	4:1; 10:11; 11:18	
Deception	12:9; 13:44; 18:23;	
	19:20	2 Thessalonians 2:7–13;
		2 Timothy 3:4, 13
Persecution	12:17; 13:7	

Levels of Reality and Action Above and Below

The book of Revelation connects a wide spectrum of action. The scope of the book covers the worlds of light and darkness (spheres of influence), good and evil moving from the throne of God to the pit of Satan. In chapter 4 John begins his elevation from the earthly Patmos to the heavenly realm of the revealing Christ. This implies that the reality of one world interacts with the reality of another world. It is also comforting to know that our concerns in the earthly realm can be addressed to God through our earthly prayers (Matthews 18:18-19).

Remember, the larger picture is more than what we see or experience. Bible events happen in time, place, and domain (spiritual and earthly). People can be affected by powers beyond themselves.

Transcendent: Heavenly, beyond this immediate world/earth. The throne, angels, elders, international and cosmic disorders, wars, etc., constitute "beyondness" played out in the world.

Local/global: Town, cities, immediate world of global society

Church/believers: The nature, the witness, accountability, is displayed in the world. Individual personality and spirituality (growth) is important to "outside" global observers. (be watchful, be strong, and be in the Word). The makeup of the saved and the unsaved (godly/ungodly, sound thinkers reprobate minds) are a part of a global mix.

The underworld:	Hell Hades	
	2 Peter 2:4	1 Peter 3:18–19; 5:8
	Isaiah 14:12–17	Jude 6, 9
	Luke 10:17–20; 16:19–25	Revelation 12:3–12; 20:1–10; 16:14

Agents of action: Forces of evil, forces of God, evil spirits, the Holy Spirit, holy angels, the living creature (beast), the dragon, fallen angels, and the Great Harlot all symbolize role, character, and influence.

The struggle: False teachers and teachings, the pressure to conform (Romans 12:1–2) and weak faith, the inability to suffer and endure, to watch and pray are present. The motivation to teach truth (a charge to all saints) and promote bonding and shared life is expected (Revelation 2:14, 15, and 20; Jude 23, 2 Thessalonians 2:10–12. The charge is to earnestly contend for the faith (Jude 3).

The church is a life-giving support system, buffer zone, faith care provider, and healing and therapeutic center. The church is an information center, an interpretation center, an outreach center, and a worship center. It is a spiritual administration/leadership center. Some believe the church will not be here during any part of the tribulation. But whenever two or three believers are found together they are, in fact, a de facto church. They are prepared to meet the bridegroom (Revelation 19:7–9). What constitutes "the church" during "end-times" has not been clearly defined or agreed to by Bible scholars.

The kinds of surroundings we interact with eventually affect us. Many people are living unstable and unsatisfied lives because they do not realize a part of their problem lies in the disorder caused by the presence of hindering influences or spirits. When children go to school, for example, they are exposed to new social vocabularies, jealousies, angry people, disturbed persons, and amoral people with questionable values. What is generally accepted is that evil has an agenda. This agenda is implied in Ephesians 6:11-12, 1 Peter 5:8, Matthew 24:4-5, and Revelation 13:7-8.

The purpose of evil in the world is:

- to confuse people about Christ and salvation.
- to corrupt human culture as an alternate source for idealistic Kingdom life.
- to resist all that is of God and divert attention from truth.
- to undermine standards of justice, truth, beauty, and valued human life.
- to create disorder, anarchy (no authority), desperation, and disunity.
- to create dysfunctional people unable to think clearly and act decisively.
- to have people live a depressed life of ambiguity (uncertainty) without purpose.
- to have people live in fear, distrust, and mental isolation (bipolar stress, pressure).
- to destroy faith on the earth.
- to corrupt institutions so that no effective good can emerge. Institutions could become tools of control, oppression, and exploitation.

Resurrection, Rapture, and Stewardship

The current hostile social-political climate has caused many people in secular society to take a look at religious concepts like prophecy, end-time conditions, the afterlife, and the question of ultimate justice coming to the world. Will it ever get better? What does the lordship and reign of Christ really mean, if anything? While believers wait, they can choose to be indifferent to world conditions and the needs of hurting people.

Unfortunately, we live in a narcissistic society of self-centered people, even among believers. It is tempting to attempt to isolate one's self and withdraw from reality. Yet, Jesus states you are the lights of the world and the salt of the earth. (Matthews 5:13-14).

("And as he sat upon the mount of Olives, the disciples came unto him privately, saying, Tell us, when shall these things be? and what shall be the sign of thy coming, and of the end of the world?" Matthew 24:3; "When they therefore were come together, they asked of him, saying, Lord, wilt thou at this time restore again the kingdom to Israel?" (Acts 1:6)

There are many views about the return of (Parousia) Christ and the suffering or non-suffering of the saints. Several scriptures refer to a coming in the clouds, resurrection, taken up, seized up (1 Thessalonians 4:14-17), tribulation, kingdom, and the day of the Lord. "But the day of the Lord will come as a thief in the night" (2 Peter 3:10), with no time line.

There are scriptures that refer to episodic events of the future but do not directly convey or connect a timetable for them. Sometimes zeal causes many to create their own timetable with questionable linkages of scriptures. (Matthew 24:29–31, 40–41; Mark 13:26–27; Luke 21:25–27; 1 Corinthians 15:20–26, 51–52; 1 Thessalonians 4:13–17; 2 Thessalonians 2:1–2, 8–9; Daniel 7:13).

"One day is with the Lord as a thousand years, and a thousand years as one day" (2 Peter 3:8). "But of that day and hour knoweth no man, no, not the angels of heaven, but my Father only" (Matthew 24:36). As we explore *Revelation Now*, our emphasis is not on the calendar of events that we cannot know in full, but on our responsibility to guard our faith, pursue justice (Isaiah 59:4, Micah 6:8), and manifest the love of God (John 13:35).

As we move on from the introduction section we shall proceed to explore the Book of Revelation in this manner. We shall examine a brief overview of the God-man (Jesus Christ) giving John revelatory insight on the seven churches, then the throne room in heaven. Believers define themselves against the background of world empires which are briefly described.

Then the unfolding of the seven seals and bowls are presented along with the witnesses, the woman – with child and beastly forces. A discussion about the affect of turbulence, the fall of Babylon the great, and the final conflict follows tribulation discussions. The book ends with victory in the final defeat of evil.

Chapter One

Direct Revelation:
The Receiving Servant

○ ○

"And if you will receive it …"

(Matthew 11:14).

In order to function at all in this complex, demanding world, we need ongoing information and understanding. We should know about the actions of people and structures that influence how things happen. What we don't know can hurt us. For example, we cannot be ignorant of the law or the right procedures concerning jobs, schools, proper foods to eat or avoid, and inclement weather conditions that affect our safety and mobility. There is some guiding information in this life that we have to know.

John used the phrase, "The revelation of Jesus Christ, which God gave unto him" (Revelation 1:1). Revelation is seen as an essential gift of information. It was direct communication. It was priceless, wireless, and spiritual. It was and is an unveiled, declassified message. This message is also a testimony and a witness about unfolding critical events. These events and Christ as the living Word work together to provide a comprehensive view about the world. This information provides a glimpse of turbulent conditions that we must face. This leads to preparation, relevant prayer, and ministry. The Word provides answers for seeking believers who want to be prepared to handle various conditions.

> The Revelation of Jesus Christ, which God gave unto him, to shew unto his servants things which must shortly come to pass; and he sent and signified it by his angel unto his servant John: Who bare record of the word of God, and of the testimony of Jesus Christ, and of all things that he saw. Blessed is he that readeth, and they that hear the words of this prophecy, and keep those things which are written therein: for the time is at hand. (Revelation 1:1–3)

The implication is that just as John received the revelation, so should those who *read and hear* the words of this prophesy keep those things that are written in it, for the time is at hand. The time is now. This does not mean that all the events will occur at the same time. It does mean that we should now receive and believe the report about that which is about to come. "Nowness" is the beginning of the unfolding of the apocalypse. Nowness is also about the relevancy of unfolding events in our own time. Now is about the symbolic Rome, Babylon, and institutionalized power of the beast (living creature) who begins to emerge. Now is the time to stand fast, endure hardship, and hear what the Spirit is saying. Believers need to engage God in a receptive mode of timely, revelatory communication. The believing person experiences a *karious* event (moment of timely inspiration). Apocalyptic conditions of the age call for a deep sense of seeing and hearing in order to avoid a lost sense of direction, devotion, and doctrine. End-time (eschatological) behavior adjustments call for a knowledge of God's will and purpose for believers who live in a fast-track, traumatic, and dramatic world. Remember, one time period subtly fades into and overlaps the next. These occurrences that creep up on us can catch us off-guard and unwatchful. Sometimes repeated trying events gradually neutralize our concern. We become numb or indifferent.

The God-Man Asserts His Presence

The identity of the one who reveals is clearly established in the first chapter. He is the one who was and who is and who is to come. This refers to the pre-existence, the present, and the future divine one, Jesus the Christ. Readers need to be reminded of the majestic, divine, and royal order of Jesus. Believers constitute his priesthood ministry.

Our perspective on Christ (our Christology) affects our prayer life, our faith level, and even our courage to face the world. Affirmation of the earthly, heavenly, and post-resurrection existence of Christ is highlighted in this chapter. He is one like the Son of man.

> I saw in the night visions, and, behold, one like the Son of man came with the clouds of heaven, and came to the Ancient of days, and they brought him near before him. (Daniel 7:13)

He appeared with priestly dress and distinction. His hair is wool-like and white, reflecting wisdom and maturity. "I beheld till the thrones were cast down, and the Ancient of days did sit, whose garment was white as snow, and the hair of his head like pure wool: his throne was like the fiery flame, and his wheels as burning fire" (Daniel 7:9). His eyes and face reflect a strong brilliance. His feet are like bronze burned in a fire. Obviously, this personal description of his appearance is deliberate. Jesus Christ is depicted in his unique human form.

> His head and his hairs were white like wool, as white as snow; and his eyes were as a flame of fire; And his feet like unto fine brass, as if they burned in a furnace; and his voice as the sound of many waters. And he had in his right hand seven stars: and out of his mouth went a sharp twoedged sword: and his countenance was as the sun shineth in his strength. (Revelation 1:14–16)

The God-man asserts his own justified sovereignty. He appears holding the seven stars in his right hand. Christ oversees the stars and they are accountable to him. The seven stars, angels, or messengers are usually considered to be the pastors or bishops of the Asia Minor churches. The sharp, two-edged sword was directed at these leaders as a timely word for evaluation, correction, and direction. God is very much in touch with his people, his ministry, and his mission. He does inform, reveal, and guide the course of the doctrine, teachings, and deeds of his earthly ambassadors. End-times calls for messengers with a liberating, timely and relevant (*rhema*) word. This word moves beyond human wisdom, motivational speeches, and political correctness.

Christ identifies himself to John as the I Am, the Alpha and Omega (first and last). John states that he is already experiencing tribulation as a companion with all others who are suffering and will suffer. He is instructed to write the vision down and send it to the seven churches of Asia Minor. He is specifically asked to send it to the leaders (angels) of these churches.

> And when I saw him, I fell at his feet as dead. And he laid his right hand upon me, saying unto me, Fear not; I am the first and the last: I am he that liveth, and was dead; and, behold, I am alive for evermore, Amen; and have the keys of hell and of death. Write the things which thou hast seen, and the things which are, and the things which shall be hereafter. (Revelation 1:17–19)

The Revelation begins by presenting one who has longevity, divine and human attributes, and eternal significance. Jesus is the key personality in this salvation drama and its final culmination. This messianic figure has been visualized in the spirit by prophets and servants of God, including David, Daniel, Joel, Jeremiah, Isaiah, Zechariah, and Malachi (Malachi 3:1–3; 4:2–3)

The presentation of the bigger picture also helps to provide the seeker with a greater sense of appreciation for these models and witnesses who endured opposition and persecution through mega structures and their representatives. Mega structures are social and political, "faceless" bureaucracies whose ruling domains are in reality difficult to negotiate. Believers create their own way of faith thinking and living in the midst of their particular situation. They redefine the meaning of life in the world as they experience it. Unique faith communities have emerged in the center of mundane cultures and empires. Believers act out a transcendent faith beyond the principalities and powers that could be intimidating.

In the process of endurance, people of faith developed a strong identity and collective consciousness. This consciousness was constantly reflected in the language and terms they used. Early converts to Christianity began to experience a different view of the world. In time they created an empire of faith based upon the liberating love of God. This strong foundational faith has led the way to global Christianity under the most trying conditions.

Oppositional, non-conforming life in the world is reflected in key terms and expressions and sense of self (selves). These terms show the new, emerging lifestyles. A faith orientation of converted believers has emerged. These terms tell us indirectly or directly what is actually going on as believers engage or disengage the world. For example, these self-defining terms gained wide usage in the early church.

Witness/Martyr: one who risks all as an act of absolute trust in Christ (Ephesians 1:12–13).

Overcome (*nikao*): a legal term that means "to prevail," but by faith to overcome evil seductions in the world. 1 John 5:4, Romans 12:21, Revelation 13:7–8; 15:2, 4

Ekklesia: called-out ones from a fallen society/world.

Remnant: faith survivors, those who regather and submit fully to God.

Teleos: ultimate purpose, goal, completion, attainment (1 Corinthians 15:24–25).

Proskuneo *(Sahah):* those who worship or bow down to God. They have chosen God and rejected gods of the culture and empire (Revelation 5:11–14).

Enmity: hostility versus friendship is seen in God versus the world paradox (Ephesians 2:13–18; James 4:4)

Pagideuo: entanglement or being woven into the fabric of this world, which is to be avoided.

Akribos: walking circumspectly, carefully in the world, or walking precisely according to your faith and God's will (Titus 3:1–4; Ephesians 5:15–16)

Renew: living a different life, a resurrected life as recovery from an old, unregenerated nature, the carnal self (Ephesians 2:15). It involves "being" in pursuit of another standard beyond the world. One strives to avoid adopting the habits and mind-set of the world.

In summation, the world as a cosmic order was seen in the sense of a godless sphere by Biblical writers. Conditions in the world reflected a fallen humanity, which was in a state of alienation and opposition to God. A new politics of identity emerged in which believers were to walk in the light of Christ, as a good citizens of society. They operated according to a higher system of belief and love. These teachings were already in place by the time the book of Revelation was written. The book presupposes a critical attitude toward the world. Early believers were expected to embrace the beatitudes despite worldly opposition. Even in the context of the empires of this world, Jesus was and is Lord (Matthew 5, Luke 6, 1 John 2:15–17; 3:10).

Never Lose Sight on the Setting: Church and Empires

All human events occur against the background of history. Biblical history was cast in a setting of seven major empires. This background presence tells us something about the scope of God's work. It also tells us about unnoticed people, factors, and motives at work. The ancient world developed military, cultural, and political nation-states that influenced the activity of biblical history and experience. All life is interrelated. During the recording of the canon books of scripture, there were many episodes that reflected an inclusive world scene in the salvation drama. Both Old and New Testament history is framed around the power of world empires and opposing ideas in the history of faith. Faith had to be developed in the context and face of adversarial persuasions and diverse cultures.

Diverse nations became symbolic, meaningful, and significant in world influence and contrast. For example, in the book of Revelation, the corrupting symbolic power of Rome and Egypt are seen as the Babylon of world culture. This view is embedded in the eschatological unfolding of the new world order. References to the dragon, the beast, and the seat of Satan involve indications of structured evil in the global context. The drama of good and evil involves principalities and the rulers of darkness in pursuit of world control and hegemony (dominating ideology).

Biblical events were born in the context of empire, dominion, and conflict. This became the center stage of historic reality. Egyptian pharaohs and Assyrian, Babylonian, and Roman rulers were a part of this drama (Daniel 6:1–5; Jeremiah 21:4). Conflicts in the book of Revelation are not regional but global. Global conflicts affect regional life and relationships. Asa, king of Judah (911–870 BCE), who was right before God, was able to defeat Zerah, the Ethiopian general, who had an army of one million soldiers and three hundred chariots at the battle of Zephathah. The Ethiopians lost the battle and a great multitude of cattle and possessions only because of God's intervention. This was the period of Ethiopia's great military might in the world. In 701 a combined force of Egypt and Ethiopia marched to join the king of Assyria as allies.

Ethiopia and Egypt were the strength of Nineveh, the capital of Assyria before 662 (Nahum 3:9). Ethiopia and Egypt symbolized a great alliance of military power. Around 663 BCE Assyria attacked and over threw Thebes in Egypt. Assyria had already defeated Israel in 722 BCE and now Assyria (Nineveh) was about to fall in 612 BCE. It is apparent that between 900 and 600 BCE Ethiopia was an active international player in this region. Hans Conzelmann (1987) a prominent scholar of the testament states that the historian Luke who wrote the book of Acts had no special interest in the geographical area of Africa. But, Luke mentions the traveling treasurer of a queen (Candance) from the Napta-Meroe city state region of Ethiopia. Conzelmann reports that Ethiopia occupied an intrigue and political spot-light in the area at that time (about 33 AD).

Conflicts between different types of belief systems that were present in Egypt, Babylon, Palestine, Syria, Greek and Roman cultures continue in the apocalypse. The major agenda of all world empires is about who shall rule and who shall be "worshiped". It is about the control of people and alliances, control of resources, and world status. This is enforced through prevailing agreements. Military threats and pacts (treaties) "There is a league between me and thee, and between my father and thy father: behold, I have sent unto thee a present of silver and gold; come and break the league with Baasha king of Israel, that he may depart from me." (1 Kings 15:19), As in Rome, conquerors held public parades, marching with captured loot, prisoners as the spoils of war and the humiliation of their lost. This represented more than a military victory. It was the visible evidence of a superior ruler, people, and culture. This is why each invading conqueror dismantled every major symbol, temple, and buildings of significance. Libraries, government buildings, city centers, statutes, and historic records were destroyed. The visible evidence of a foe's civilization was eradicated. Adversaries loved to erase and remove signs of competition, rival greatness, or even existence. For instance, the Egyptians left little or no deliberate evidence that the Hebrews were in their country for four hundred years and left victoriously.

Seven Biblical Empires

Interacting Civilizations	Pre-State	Empire Reign	Leadership Figures
Egypt	5500 BCE	3150–525 BCE	Abram 2166–1991 BCE
Ethiopia/Kush	8000 BCE	1000 BCE–AD 100	Moses 1526–1406 BCE
Babylon	3000 BCE	2000–539 BCE	Saul 1051–1011 BCE
Assyria	2600 BCE	729–612 BCE	David 1011–971 BCE
Indo-Mede (Persia)	1000 BCE	550–330 BCE	Solomon 971–931 BCE
Greek	1400 BCE	332–30 BCE	Hosaea/Israel/Isaiah 758-722 BCE
Roman	753/509 BCE	29 BCE–AD 476	Zedekiah/Jeremiah 586 BCE
	Transitional	Period	
Exile/Return Period	586 BCE Babylon	536 BCE Persia Daniel 620–540	Ezra 458 BCE Nehemiah 444 BCE
Christ's advent 6–4 BCE	Death on the cross AD 30	Book of Acts written AD 64–65	Augustus Caesar 27 BCE–AD 14

Ethiopian Traveling Treasurer AD 33	Paul's call AD 35	Paul's first missionary journey AD 45	Domitianus AD 81–96; Revelation written AD 95

Note: Ancient countries had no clear-cut boundaries, beginning dates and precise identities. History is an unfolding process. Dates are subject to sources, interpretations, and persuasions of the researcher and the times. Archeological study is still in process.

Historic nation-states had these characteristics in common: a developed history, an organized government, system of law, a strong, organized military, a well-defined culture, a developed agriculture trade beyond its immediate borders, and international influence. Some of the nation-states were very old and achieved their empire status later in their history. Some of them had more than one great historic, cultural, and military period. All of them had to be taken seriously by their contemporaries. Their area of dominion was well established during their reign of greatness.

Biblical History: the World of Aggressive Empires

Ethiopia/Kush

Ethiopia was old and unassuming in the historic library of who is who in world civilizations. It was and still is ignored by some historians, believers and non-believers. The ancient Kushites were descendants from an Afro-Asiatic-speaking people who dwelt in northeast Africa. Today that area would include Sudan, Ethiopia, Eritrea, and Somalia. It included a large territory at the time. The same wide geographical area gave rise to a people who are reported to have lived about 180,000 BCE. The humans in East Africa eventually became a definable people in and around 60,000 BCE. Early Kush was supported by localized hunting and food gathering. Later, it was known for its trading in gold. The area surrounded the lower Nile Valley was also called Abbay, the Blue Nile, and Gihon in Genesis 2:13 that flowed around the whole land of Kush. The river Gihon was described as winding or flowing all through the land of Kush. At that time the land encompassed a greater area. This area would include, but not be limited to Abbay, the lower Nile Valley. Genesis 2:13 emphasizes "the whole land of Kush" obviously we do not know what that means today. The picture is complicated because of the reference to the Euphrates River which usually means a location in Assyria. However, Assyria was not known to have had significant gold deposits. Also the Nile Valley was considered to be a rich favorite area long before others were known. Usually areas that border rivers are ideal for vegetation. In this case a garden or paradise kind of environment would have to have had a natural, luscious, over abundance of plants, trees, herbs, and exotic botanical life. This could be a model similar to the great Amazon River area in Brazil. It may not be for us to know the exact location of Eden, but to appreciate the symbolism of its existence. In addition we know little about the original geography of the area and any geographical shifts that may have occurred.

There were favorable environmental conditions until 16,000 BCE, when the level of rain, rain forest, woodlands, and grasslands decreased. About 13,000–11,000 BCE, the climate changed again and vegetation increased, and so did the population. This change helped to support the emergence of an organized people able to thrive. At about the same period there was an increase in agricultural development, stone tools, administration, civic society, and language development (8,000 BCE). The proto Afro-Asiatic (forerunner) language split into Kushantic speech and Omotic- and Chadic-related languages. The Ethiopic language predates ancient Arabic well over one thousand years, around 15,000–8000 BCE. Language was spoken before it was written. Rosa paintings were found dating to 10,000 BCE.

By 3500 BCE, wheat, barley, fishing, and irrigation were in full use. Eventually the people increased their domestication of sheep, goats, donkeys, and cattle. Stone bowls and pottery were used to hold grain porridge. Cereal agriculture also started in the north region of Ethiopia. Kush had pharaonic tombs in 3800 to 3100 BCE. By 1700 to 600 BCE, it became a major trading nation. Edwin Yamarchi reports that from 1700 to 1500 BCE, Kush became a powerful, wealthy state. Their expert weapon was the mighty bow. Kush developed thriving grain agriculture including barley and wheat. Iron tools for farms and war dykes and irrigation channels were developed. Kush has 223 pyramids in Mere and Napatal (more than Egypt, but not as large). It had an advanced 260-day calendar.

Kush also had a well developed system of government. They had outstanding kings and Nubian queens. Thriving cities were developed. These included Axum, Meroe the city-state, later the center of iron smelting, Napata, Kerma, and Shendi, a sister town. The Ethiopians were scholars in geography, astronomy, and time measurement. More about Kush is being discovered after years of historic and excavation neglect and indifference.

By 1000 BCE, Kush had conquered the entire region below Kemet (Egypt) and became an empire. In 2 Kings 19:8 and 2 Chronicles 14:9–14, there are references to the great period of Ethiopian reign and influence.

The historian Josephus, along with Origen and Jerome, members of Kush/Ethiopian church fathers, and Ethiopians stated that the 1 Kings account of the queen of Sheba refers to an Ethiopian queen (Felder 1989). The story dating from the reign of Solomon (962–922 BCE) reflects the wealth and status of the Nubian dynasty at the same period of its greatest height. It does not reflect Sheba as an Arab source in this visitation. Jesus called her the "queen of the south" and not the east (Matthew 12:42).

Ethiopia consisted of many city-states adjoining Kushite areas to form one empire. Empire status according to scholars includes a large land area, centralized administration, a formal army, a definable culture, international influence, and trade. The Aksumite kingdom moved from city-state to empire status over a long period of time. It prospered from high trade from caravan traffic and the Nile valley. Ethiopia also excelled in architecture, coinage, and administration until AD 300. The kingdom declined rapidly after the rise and influence of Islam and its increased control over the area's trade. The Arabs were aggressive traders, politicians, and slave merchants.

The ancient Ethiopian empire spanned about 1000 BCE to about 100 BCE. During this period the Ethiopians had been invaded by Egypt many times but also had a presence in Egypt in the eleventh and eighteenth dynasties before the Kushite (twenty-fifth) dynasty, which formally started about 775 to 656 BCE. They ruled effectively in Egypt during the twenty-fifth dynasty for 104 years. Egyptian records show that heavy, ongoing trade occurred between Ethiopia and Egypt for many years. This included the land of Punt or northeast

Nubia, which today is Eritrea and Somalia. Trade included gold, ivory, and wood. Ezekiel warned Israel that Ethiopia was one of those powerful nations that they needed to be prepared for (Ezekiel 38:5–7). There are many references to Ethiopia or Kush in the Bible, including Genesis 2:13 and 10:7; 2 Kings 19:8–13; 2 Chronicles 14:9–13; Daniel 11:43; Psalm 68:31 and 87:4; Ezekiel 29:10 and 38:5; Nahum 3:9; Isaiah 11:11; 20:3; 37:9; Jeremiah 38:7; and Acts 8:27.

Egypt/Kemet/Mizraim

The civilization of Egypt is so well known that its unique place in history is without parallel. The name *Kemet* means the "black land," the valley of the Nile in ancient Egyptian. The first Egyptian proto-dynasty existed between 3400 and 2686 BCE. The basic agricultural, economic, and political institutes were developed during the pre-dynastic period, which was 5500–3050 BCE. By 1000 BCE it was on the decline.

Egypt was advanced in every known category of human achievement: agriculture, irrigation, astronomy, mathematics, history, government, judiciary, military, art, international relations, architecture, religious theology, and a structured society. Egyptian philosophical theory formed a basis for early philosophy, well known to visiting ancient Greeks. Egypt contained great administrators. There were thirty-three dynasties, or ruling houses.

King Narmer unified Egypt in 3150 BCE. The old kingdom existed 2686–2181. The first great pharaohs built their pyramids in 2575–2180. The middle kingdom lasted from 2040 to 1782. The new kingdom (1570–1070) pyramids were built in 1530–1020. The period of 1279–1212 is considered by some scholars to include the reign of Ramses II of the Exodus and nineteenth dynasty. The new kingdom was from 1570–1085, and the resurgent kingdom lasted from 750–590.

About 1280 BCE the Egyptians won a great battle at Kadesh (Syria) against the Hittites, which led to the collapse of the Hittite nation. The period of 767–671 BCE is known as the period of the Black Pharaohs. This was a period when a series of rulers of Nubian descent conquered and reigned over Egypt.

Tirhaka, king of the Ethiopians, was one of the ruling pharaohs from the twenty-fifth Egyptian dynasty, about 760–656 BCE. The

Israelites wanted Tirhaka's army to challenge an anticipated assault by Sennacherib of Assyria. The Assyrians invaded lower Egypt in 670 BCE. The Kushites retreated to Nubia to build a powerful kingdom. Aksumite the Assyrian ruled Egypt from 667–652 BCE.

In 525 BCE the Persians invaded Egypt. From 322–30 BCE, Greek kings ruled Egypt. In the year 30 BCE, Egypt was occupied by imperial Rome. The country was important because it served as the great crossroad between the Middle East and sub-Saharan Africa. It also provided the Asiatic corridor for trade and culture with its European neighbors.

Assyria

The Assyrian empire emerged out of Babylonian, Hittite, and Hurrian cultures. Assyria began as a Sumerian (united) culture about 2600–2000 BCE. The Babylonians ruled Assyria from 1920 to 1850, as the Babylonian empire was in decline. After the Hittites were weakened in battle at Kadesh (Syria) by the Egyptians in 1280 BCE, Assyria took over the void of leadership. Around 900 BCE, it became an expanding empire. Assyria under King Tiglath-Pileser III defeated the Babylonians in 729 BCE. About 734 BCE, Tiglath (called Pul in 2 Kings 15:19) prevailed over Israel (King Menahem 745–738 of Israel) and Syria. He received tribute from Syrian princes and Israel, which had to raise taxes on the wealthy. That brought resentment and revolt. Tiglath conquered Damascus 732 and became king of Babylon in 729 BCE.

About 722 BCE, Sargon II took both Samaria and Carchemish. About 724 BCE King Hoshea, the last king of Israel, refused to pay tribute to Shalmanese V, as Menahem had done with Tiglath, and was deposed from his throne. There was a mass deportation of 27,290 Israelites when Assyria conquered Samaria. The area was repopulated by Babylonian colonists. In 705, Sennacherib (who worshiped Nisrach, his god) took Sion and defeated Egypt as Egypt, Babylon, and Syria plotted and incited unrest in Palestine. In 689 he destroyed Babylon, but he was assassinated in 681.

In 612 BCE, the neo-Babylonian/Chaldean (Medes) empire destroyed Nineveh and divided up the Assyrian empire. Neco defeated Josiah, who fought in the valley of Megiddo and died in 609. But

King Neco lost to Nebuchadnezzar in 605. The defeat of Pharaoh Neco at Carchemish by Babylon made Judea a ward of Babylon until the Persians took over in 536, and later the Greeks.

Babylon

The original Babylonian civilization was a gradual product of a mixed (unknown) people and the language of the Sumerian culture (about 3500 BCE). The Mesopotamian area extended northeast, east of Syria and north of the Persian Gulf. It excelled in social order and government administration. It was famous for its writing system, mathematics, the Hammurabi Code, architecture, economics, art, and literature. The language used was from an Akkadian and Semitic mixture.

Babylon became a major metropolis of city-states and international power from 2900 to 1595 BCE. Its god was Marduk, along with Enlil, later called Bel or Lord. Human sacrifices were made. King Sargon of Aklad developed a Mesopotamian empire in 2334 BCE. Hammurabi, the sixth king, established a Babylonian empire in 1792 after many conquests. The Hittites destroyed Babylon and ruled all of Mesopotamia for 450 years beginning in 1595 BCE. About 1200 BCE, the Hittites themselves were overrun by foreign invaders. Nebuchadnezzar I over ran the Elamites, but fell to the Assyrians about 1123 BCE. In 586 BCE, Nebuchadnezzar II (605–562) captured Jerusalem. Nabanidus spent his time (555–538) in a great rebuilding program during the time of Belshazzar, his co-ruler.

In 612 BCE, the Babylonians obtained their independence from the Assyrians, who were in political chaos. Cyrus the Great of Persia easily conquered Babylon in 539 BCE during the reign of Belshazzar. Alexander the Great then captured Babylon in 332. In 312 BCE, dynasty heirs of the Seleucids became the new rulers of Babylon.

The Hebrew Bible tells us that Abraham came from Haran in northwestern Mesopotamia (Genesis 11:31). Haran is located near Balilch and Edessa and a tributary of the Euphrates River. This area, called Paddan-Aram, is mentioned in Genesis 25:20 and 28:2. Ur of the Chaldeans, the birthplace of Abraham, was said to be near Sumer in southern Mesopotamia. The biblical image of Babylon is a global symbol of culture and affluence without moral restraint and military might without mercy. Babylon is seen as a center of pagan theology and worship of the storm god, Teshub. It is a state ruled by fear and yet held in great admiration. It is known for its beastly global influence for all times. But Babylon was doomed to collapse.

Medes/Persians

The Medes (Iran) and Persians (Iraq) are considered together because of their close association and dealings with each other. Eventually the Medes became dominant and they merged. The nomadic tribes came together in 550 BCE when Cyrus the great rebelled against the ruling Medes Cyrus II governed Persia 559–530 BCE and made Media the first province of the Persian empire. He was followed by his son Cambyses (530–522) and then the Darius dynasty, which ruled until Alexander the Great in 330 BCE.

During 612 BCE, the Medes and Babylonians, who had increased in military and political strength, sacked Nineveh and destroyed Assyria. Neco, pharaoh of Egypt, was defeated in 609 after he had tried to join the Assyrians to defeat the Babylonians, but he lost to King Nebuchadnezzar II of Babylon (605–562). Neco's successors also failed in their invasion of lower Nubia. Apries (588–569 BCE) failed against Nebuchadnezzar when he tried to seize Jerusalem. Egypt came under the rule of the Persians after the defeat of Pasamtik III by Cambyses in 525 BCE. Darius the Mede reorganized the empire and made Persepolis the capital.

Daniel prophesied in Babylon during the reign of Nebuchadnezzar II, Darius the Mede, and Cyrus the Persian. Ezekiel prophesied (593–571) in Babylon during the reign of Nebuchadnezzar. Cyrus the Great (558–539) was a great military strategist and administrator. His family continued his rule and extended his empire. Cyrus conquered Persia (Iran), Lydia, and Babylon from Egypt to India. Darius, from the same dynasty, created a strong nation and reigned from 522 to 486 BCE. This dynasty ruled until 330, when Alexander the Great overcame the empire. Much of this area fell to Islam in AD 651.

Greece

The pre-Hellenic people in the area of Crete and the Aegean Islands began to unify around 4000 BCE. They were influenced by Egypt in their development. Travelers from the Aegean civilization wrote about both the Ethiopian (Kush) and Egyptians in distinct ways. Historians have demonstrated this exchange between the emerging Hellenistic culture and African nations (Asante, 2007). The Minoans (2000 BCE), a sea-fearing trading people, traded with Syria, Egypt, Libya, and Mesopotamia. They interacted with literate societies, and the Minoans themselves developed a progressive administration, records, a strong hierarchy, and selected sites for city-states, such as Athens and Pylos. The Mycenaean civilization of Argos, or mainland Greece, lasted from 1600 to 1150 BCE.

The formal emergence of the Greek civilization started in 776 BCE, the year of the first Olympic Games. Early Greek writing seemed to be an adaptation of the Phoenician alphabet and script. In time, the Greeks developed classical mythology, drama, literature, religion, poetry, art, philosophy, and famous city-states. The Greeks developed an advanced group of elite persons who led their civilization to a relatively high level of accomplishment. Greeks had slaves, most of whom were women. Later, fewer males were killed after a war and were instead put into slavery. There were not massive plantations in Greece but rather households of one or two slaves. The Greeks did not make an institution out of slavery. Greek craftsmen served in other nearby countries like Babylon.

There were more than 150 city-states. The most famous were Athens, Sparta, Argos, Thebes, and Olympia. Sparta was conservative, law-minded, and resistant to change. It had a counsel of elderly men, five magistrates and two limited "kings." These served as oligarchs. The city-states, including Athens, were ruled by aristocracies. At times there were conflicts between classes. Public life in the city (Polis) was usually conducted at the Agora, the center for secular news and cultural life. It was the marketplace for the exchange of ideas. Athens was a strong trader in oil, wine, and grain.

The last tyrant was disposed of in 510 BCE, when a more democratic Hellenistic government was instituted. The majority of votes ruled, but at the same time Athens had more slaves than other city-states. In other words, the progressive democratic tendencies did not extend to a vast number of slaves who were often considered to be a part of the family life and functioning of the Greek family. The birth of modern democracy began in Athens about 550 BCE. The political process involved the vote of the *ecclesia* (assembly). Even though the Greeks believed in democracy, the governance of the Polis ended up as the rule of an elite group of free men. Women were removed from almost all public life were believed to be inferior to men. They could not vote, own property or move about without a male guardian. They could supervise the work of family slaves.

One of the greatest triumphs of the Greeks was its victory over Persia in 490 BCE in the Battle of Marathon and again in 480 BCE. In 360 BCE, Philip II took the rule of a country in chaos, brought order by defeating his foreign enemies, and instituting internal reform, and became a respected leader beyond his home base in Macedonia. Wars continued between Persia and Greece. Philip was assassinated in 336 BCE by a member of his own bodyguard. His last wife (number seven) was a noble family woman named Cleopatra.

Alexander the Great, the son of Philip II, launched a twenty-thousand-mile military campaign over much of the known world. He defeated Darius III in 333 BCE at the Battle of Issus in Cilicia, Egypt, Iran, and India. Alexander died in 323 in Babylon at the age of thirty-three from a fever. Before he died there was much mistrust and collusion among his officers and soldiers. By 168 BCE, the Romans occupied Macedonia and most of the Mediterranean.

Rome

Myth says that Rome was founded in 753 BCE. The republic was officially founded in 590 BCE. This date may be unreliable. In 509 BCE, after the Etruscans were evicted from the territory, Rome built its own city-state after the classical Greek city-state. Rome took over Italy by 295 BCE. From 200 to 50 BCE, Roman domination covered parts of Asia. The empire fell in AD 476.

The following Roman emperors, Caesars, and rulers reigned around New Testament times (Jesus, Paul, and John the Revelator).

All dates are approximate and vary according to historians and archeological findings:

Julius, 59–44 BCE
Herod the Great, 37-4 BCE, king of Judea
Tiberius, AD 14–37
Caligula, Gaius AD 37–41
Claudius, Tibius AD 41–54
Augustus, 27 BCE–AD 14
Octavius, 27 BCE–AD 14, first emperor of Rome
Claudius, 41 BCE–AD 54
Pontius Pilate, AD 26–36, procurator of Judea
Nero, AD 54–68. The senate declared Nero a public enemy, and
   he committed suicide outside of Rome.
Galba, Servius Sulpicius, AD 68–69
Otho, AD 69
Vitellius, AD 69
Vespasianus, Titus Flavius, AD 69–79
Domitianus, Titus Flavus, AD 81–96
Nerva, Marcus Cocceius, AD 96–98
Traianus, Marcus Ulpius, AD 98–117. He died after crushing a
   Jewish revolt.

An overview of the Roman emperors presents a succession of ongoing intrigue: betrayal, conspiracy, murders, mistrust, treachery, and sometimes emotional instability among family, friends, and foes. It is an administrative marvel that the republic lasted 450 years. One major problem in the empire was the lack of a consistent means of succession. Outstanding administrators and leaders like Augustus Claudius and Domitianus made significant operational improvements. And a well-developed and disciplined army was able to lose battles yet win wars, a testimony to great leadership training and field strategies. In addition Rome instituted building programs and world outreach, roads and the *pax Romana* (Roman peace).

There was also emphasis on emperor worship by a number of Caesars. A strong empire demanded loyalty to the Roman republic and ruling Caesars from the city-states and local governments in the empire. This continued until the empire gradually became corrupt and disintegrated. Domitianus advocated moral reform during his fifteen-year reign but wanted to be known as the god-king.

The Romans had a high regard for advanced civilizations. They used Greek slaves as mentors and artisans. They made agreements with those they conquered and permitted many to become Roman citizens. Some historians say that the Romans presided over a largely Hellenistic world dominated by the republic. The Romans sought to establish a universal common law, maintain peace in the empire, and utilize local culture to create a cosmopolitan empire using good administration and taxes as a strong fiscal base. Peace often came to the Roman administration because of quiet acquiescence. Non-rebellious nations and provinces subject to the intimidations of such a great empire merely gave in without a fight.

Interactions by these empires with biblical countries varied during particular points in history. For example, Isaiah the prophet declared the downfall of two empires, Ethiopia and Egypt:

> Woe to the land shadowing with wings, which is beyond the rivers of Ethiopia: That sendeth ambassadors by the sea, even in vessels of bulrushes upon the waters, saying, Go, ye swift messengers, to a nation scattered and peeled … a people terrible from their beginning hitherto… The burden of Egypt, Behold, the LORD rides upon a swift cloud, and shall come into Egypt: and the idols of Egypt shall be moved at his presence … So shall the king of Assyria lead away the Egyptians prisoners, and the Ethiopians captives, young and old, naked and barefoot, even with their buttocks uncovered, to the shame of Egypt. And they shall be afraid and ashamed of Ethiopia their expectation, and of Egypt their glory. Isaiah 18:1–2; 19:1; 20:4–5

The presence of the major empire players on the ancient world stage is often read but not seen as significant. This chapter uses the Biblical account of what is called "Salvation history" and examines this account in light of a greater frame of reference. This composite picture helps us to take notice of some information that is not normally taken seriously or seen as a part of the interaction of faith, religion and history.

Chapter Two

The Seven Churches as Centers of Lost Influence

The placement of these seven churches in the beginning of Revelation is strategic. The real-life experiences of these churches mirror the drama of empire influence and world culture. These churches are projections of the struggles to come with the "gods" of this world and structures of power. The future is always seen in light of the past and present. Everything is connected. The trend of culture and religious syncretism continues from Old Testament challenges with idols and Baal worship. Human and world practices tend to perpetuate themselves, so it is not difficult to observe emerging patterns and potential clashes (Matthew 13:14; 2:3; Ephesians 5:15–17; 2 Timothy 3:1, 13).

Simple, localized matters can indicate international trends. It is important to examine brief profiles of seven local churches that are linked to global events in the coming future. The challenges, conflicts, and weaknesses of these seven churches are real-life challenges for all churches. These churches eventually faded into history. In times to come, it will be difficult to survive as a faith community in the cosmic struggle with forces of organized evil.

These church experiences are placed early in the book so that the reader will be more prepared to move from a concrete "case study" assessment to a more abstract projection of universal testing. A new reality will come when men's hearts will fail and lives will be thrown into chaos. The reader is flung into future situations of principalities and powers operating on a grand scale. Yet, for the believer, God remains a constant source of love, comfort, and deliverance. This reality is seen in a prayerful, obedient faith community.

Greetings to the Seven Churches: High Expectations

This passage has been written because Jesus Christ, the faithful witness envisions a high view and critical role for the church in the world. Therefore, the greetings to these churches and the world contain a noble tone of majestic accountability.

To   Ephesus:
From: He that holds the seven stars (church leaders) as celestial representatives in his right hand and walks in the midst of the seven golden candlesticks (churches). 2:1

To   Smyrna:
From: The first and the last, who was dead and is alive. (He who is the resurrection and the life, who was before any of his adversaries. Christ is the new order.) 2:8

To   Pergamos:
From: He who has the sharp sword with two edges (the power of the rational intellect on one side and the mighty one of retribution and judgment on the other side) 2:12, cutting between belief and unbelief, truth and deception, carnal and spiritual (Hebrews 4:12).

To   Thyatira:
From: The Son of God (co-ruler God) who has flaming eyes and fine brass feet (sharp, comprehensive vision, sense of direction, strength of standing with zeal and vitality). The Son stands in contrast to the local deity. 2:18

To   Sardis:
From: He who has the seven spirits of God and the seven stars (omniscience and leaders who are subject to Him). 3:1

To   Philadelphia:
From: He who is holy, true, and has the key of David; he who opens and no one shuts and shuts and no one opens. He is the majestic God of opportunity, authority and the possibilities of faith. He controls history. 3:7

To   Laodicea:

From: The Amen, the faithful and true witness, the beginning
        of the creation of God. (The true witness as the divine
        confirmer of all truth, as in, "Let it be so, Amen." He is
        not a cult or institutional Roman god. He is the original
        source and co-Creator God, to whom all glory, is due.) 3:14

The Churches in Context: a View from the Outside

The context of the Asia Minor church is strikingly similar to today's
world scene. The churches were a part of a city-state structure. Each
city would be called a global city today. The communal and cultural
significance of each city went beyond its local setting. These cities
represented a measure of success and autonomy. In some way each
city was tied into the empire of the Roman world. They had allegiances
and obligations to Rome, to which they were subservient. Rome was
the standard for the good, noble, and civilized world.

The churches were at the same time related to the Eastern
world and its Hellenistic culture, operating outside of Rome in faith
opposition to its god-king rulers. This situation put some social and
political pressure on the churches to cooperate with empire customs
or resist Roman culture. They had to overcome this faith conflict.
They had to choose to become "hot or cold." They had to exhibit a
firm devotion to the work of their "first love." 3:15-16 They had to
resist persecution, pressure, and worldly influence. Churches were
mandated to resist religious deception and apostasy and to know
what the Spirit was saying. It has always been a necessity to hear the
message of the spirit and to know the will of God.

The Seven Churches: Significant but Accountable, a Standard for Future Self-Reflection

The seven churches of Asia were being held accountable by the one
who lives and speaks. Specifically, the chief leaders, or angels of the
churches, were called to account for their leadership and stewardship.
By this time, the churches had some history, a track record. The
weight of responsibility is laid upon those who are called to the task

of interpreting and proclaiming the gospel of the Kingdom. The theological and practical work of the church in the world had to be accomplished according to the will and Word of God, not the political culture.

Each church community was significant in its own context. Each obviously had a charge they were expected to keep. The witness of the church was of immense importance.

> I charge thee therefore before God, and the Lord Jesus Christ, who shall judge the quick and the dead at his appearing and his kingdom; Preach the word; be instant in season, out of season; reprove, rebuke, exhort with all longsuffering and doctrine. For the time will come when they will not endure sound doctrine; but after their own lusts shall they heap to themselves teachers, having itching ears; And they shall turn away their ears from the truth, and shall be turned unto fables. But watch thou in all things, endure afflictions, do the work of an evangelist, make full proof of thy ministry. (2 Timothy 4:1–5)

Ephesus

Ephesus was the greatest of the seven churches. John is reported to have had a close relationship with this church. He is reported by some writers to have emigrated from Palestine to Ephesus where he shared his testimony before his exile to Patmos.

The city was founded in 140 BCE in western Asia Minor (now Turkey). It held a seat of proconsular government. It had a major port on the Aegean gulf for trade. Ephesus also had a great marketplace, library, gymnasiums, and a major theater that held twenty-five thousand people. Ephesus was granted self-rule by Rome in 133 BCE. It was previously under the rule of Greece and Persia. It had more than 250,000 people and a dynamic urban environment.

In religion, Ephesus was a center for the cult of Artemis and her temple. It had a reputation for magic and lucky charms. The temples of Hestin, Serapis, and Zeus also were located in Ephesus. Both Paul and Timothy labored in that city (Acts 18:19; 19:1–20; 1 Timothy 1:3). God wrought special miracles by Paul right in the pagan context.

The main criticism of the church was unmanifested love in ministry to the world. It had ceased to become the witnessing church.

Smyrna

The city was located twenty-five miles north of Ephesus near the southeast shore of the Aegean gulf. It was founded about 1000 BCE by the Greeks. A large and beautiful city, it was well organized and established. The city was rebuilt several times after being destroyed by foes. It named its temple in honor of Dea Roma (goddess of Rome). The city had a strong relationship with Rome and fostered a pluralistic pagan society.

Many Jews lived in Smyrna who had problems with the presence of the church. Historians indicate that the Jews complained to local authorities that the church was proselytizing through false doctrine. The church had gone through a lot of persecution by the hands of the government, informers, and false religious leaders. The church had more than its share of martyrs. It also had internal and external problems with infiltrators and slanders.

Pergamum

Pergamum, a capital city, was located about forty miles north of Smyrna. The name *Pergamum* means "citadel." Pergamum was once a Hellenistic cultural center (300 BCE). The city was the site of a temple built in honor of the Emperor Augustus. There was also an elevated statute of Zeus with monuments to Athena, Dionysus, and Asclepieum, the serpent god of healing. The Pergamene Church had to resist the power of Rome and the imperial cult.

Thyatira

The city was founded by Seleucus, a Macedonian general, about 300 BCE. It was considered a Macedonian settlement before 300 BCE. Little is known about the prior history of Thyatira. It was located between Pergamum and Sardis. It was captured and used as a military outpost and fell to the Romans in 190 BCE. Its position made it convenient for trade, communications, slaves, banking, manufacturing, travel, and syncretistic religion. The city had a guild for almost every trade in its society. Guild members were expected to pay homage to the designated pagan gods. Most guilds had a patron deity. Therefore, the church had to be more selective about selecting and permitting certain teachers. Interestingly, this church, in the least important city of the seven cities mentioned, received the longest message to the churches.

Sardis

Sardis was located fifty miles east of Ephesus in a strategic mountain position. Succeeding kings ruled the city, from Croesus in the sixth century BCE to the Seleucids and then to Rome in 133 BCE. The city was dedicated to Artemis, a local Greek god during the reign of Croesus. The Emperor Tiberius gave the city generous support to rebuild after a major earthquake in AD 17. Sardis was at its height in gold, silver, and wealth in the sixth century BCE, but by the time of the Romans, the city was in a sharp economic decline. It was also subject to strong Jewish and Hellenistic influence.

The church was admonished to strengthen its good practices and not let them die.

Philadelphia

This city (modern Aleshehir) was built on elevated ground about thirty miles southeast of Sardis about 189–139 BCE. Like some of the other cities, its location made it a convergent point for trade, agriculture, and some industry. It is reported that the city's name reflected the close association between Attalus and Eumenes, two brothers. Philadelphia, like Sardis, was hit with a major earthquake around AD 17. Since Philadelphia was located in a great vineyard area, its pagan god was Dionysus, the god of wine. The city, like Sardis, was subject to strong Judaizing and Hellenistic influence. Both of these cultures were promoted in the city.

Bishop Polycarp and other Christians from Philadelphia were martyred. Yet, this church exhibited great love and patience.

Laodicea

Laodicea was founded about 261–246 BCE by Antiochus II, whose wife's name was Laodice. The city was connected by trade routes: Ephesus to the west, Pergamum to the South, and a northern route to the other five cities mentioned in the letter. Laodicea was the most wealthy, prosperous, and independent city in the area. It was well known for its banking industry, commercial agricultural and administrative centers. It housed a famous medical school. The school was associated with the pagan cult of the god-men. In the second century Laodicea became a meeting place for philosophers.

Antioch was southeast of Laodicea. Athens lay to the west, across the Mediterranean Sea from Ephesus. Jerusalem was south of Ephesus and Colosse; both were one hundred miles east of Laodicea and Antioch. These cities reflect, more or less, the evangelistic routes of Paul and the apostles in the book of Acts. Across the Mediterranean Sea from Ephesus was Corinth to the south and Philippi and Thessalonica to the north (in Macedonia). The churches in these cities were fairly connected in terms of adjacent regions. Some historians believe that Laodicea had a large Jewish population.

This church needed to renounce self-pride, independence, and indifference. Total dependence on Christ was a necessity despite the affluence of their day.

Divine Rebuke

The matter of addressing the seven churches is critical. If the churches were vibrant and fully alive, they would not need such a direct confrontation and divine rebuke. There was a spiritual tension between faith and works, the world of God and the world of the empire culture. Each of the seven angels (messengers, leaders) was held responsible for the spirit and performance of each church. The Lord made it clear that he was very much present and aware of church life and church trials. He knew about the exhaustive labor and active deceivers in Ephesus and Smyrna, two cities that rivaled each other for greatness and were allied with Rome. Even Pergamum was devoted to the Romans. Comments for Ephesians and Smyrna included "impostor," "poverty," "prison confinement," "witness," and "endurance." The Smyrneans were greatly exploited because the Christian faith was illegal. This led to great poverty, and some were martyred. In the context of an evil, a pluralistic society of competing religious persuasions, there was conflict with both pagans and Jews.

The Lord, who searches all minds and hearts, was fully aware of the location and activity of Satan's false doctrine, spiritual fornication, and the need for the church to repent. The church's failure to control and monitor teachers and teaching was sharply rebuked, which means that teaching and interpreting the gospel is viewed as a serious matter. On the other hand, significant rewards for maintaining a vibrant, proven witness are promised to effective believers.

The mission of the churches involved serious responsibilities supported by sound doctrine. The church in Thyatira, for instance, needed to fully understand the magnitude of Satanic devices and influence. The church in Sardis needed to be watchful and strengthen those vital practices and works that were falling apart (Sardis). The Lord even warned the church at Sardis that he would intervene suddenly and come upon an unrepentant, wavering church that was ineffective in its mission. Clearly, the role of the church in the world, regardless of conditions, is important to God.

The church at Philadelphia had kept the Word with patience and would be undergirded during the "hour of temptation" to be present in the known world, whenever that is. God has an open door for those who have invested their strength and will be able to look forward to the ultimate coming of the New Jerusalem. The one who has the key of David and is holy will stamp God's name upon his overcomers. This is in direct contrast to the church of Laodicea, which preferred to be neutral or lukewarm. The church that feels it has everything actually is poor, miserable, blind, and naked, Jesus said. The one that loves them chastens and rebukes them to encourage repentance. If they have the voice of the Spirit, they will open their eyes, hear with their ears, and cover their weaknesses.

Did They Matter?

The seven churches represent the organized witness of Christian believers in the historic context of Asia Minor. Revelation chapters two and three help to show how they responded to challenging circumstances. The social-political environment creates conditions that affect how people think and act. The personal faith disposition of believers together help to determine how they are going to respond to opposing powers that operate in any given area.

The churches should fully understand the deceiving nature of evil in the world.

Nevertheless all believers must reflect the justice and mercy of God in their own faith organizations. They know the kingdoms of the world operate in greed, mistrust, and in power struggles. Therefore, believers must be careful to avoid the appearance of evil, selfish motives when operating through not-for-profit and missionary ministries.

Obviously, the matter of accountability is important. It becomes especially important in regard to the well-being of the people, perfecting leadership, and witness in the world. The public evidence or witness of the authenticity of the gospel of Jesus Christ must be maintained (John 17:21). There is a tendency even for believers to be co-opted by powerful institutions. The indulgences of money, affluence, and celebrity status can help neutralize significant witness in the world. That's why there is always a cloud of observing witnesses present to observe the integrity and cohesion of the faith community (Hebrews 12:1).

The concerns of the writer of Revelation were not limited to the seven churches but all churches in time and history. The nations and people of the earth are held accountable in his book. All must repent. In fact, all nations, all people, and all unjust transactions in the world system are accountable to God, whether they know it or not.

Future Concerns

The challenges of the seven churches are indicators of future global experiences. Most ministry and outreach efforts occur through groups of believers with similar commitments.

Good group personality traits include self-sacrifice, patience, and fairness, intolerance to evil, discernment, love, and spiritual sensitivity. Believers should not ignore group conflict, discord, or false worship. The message that is communicated in Revelation and others is one of exposure to false political views, doctrine, and alliances.

Believers are made aware of false teachers and arrogant, swelling words. The biblical theme of unjust imprisonment and betrayal is also prominent (Revelation 2:10; John 16:2; Acts 5:18; Hebrews 11:36).

High Influence Centers

Each of the seven churches represented centers of high influence in the eastern Roman Empire. These were noted for their strategic trade routes, rivers, fertile valleys, political - administrative centers, manufacturing-commercial activities, military outposts, harbors, marketplaces, amphitheaters, temples, and libraries, schools of philosophy, medicine, and cultural exchange. In this context, there was a special need for a strong witness for each of these churches. There was no time for anything else. They required a complete Christian witness for these high-profile cities. It is the will of God that pagan centers of unbelief are transformed and replaced by a complete manifestation of the true God. Centers of unbelief should become centers of truth and spiritual worship as churches operate in truth and transparency.

These churches were present in areas that had their own god centers. Each church stood in contrast to an opposing traditional god cult and pagan belief system. There were representative gods at these god centers for each district, and many worshiped more than one god. (Their names may have different spellings depending upon the reference.) This was the time for churches to shine in these areas of pagan belief. However, something happened and eventually the glitter disappeared. Be aware of churches with glitter and no life-giving substance.

God Centers and Temples

Ephesus   Artemis or Diana, called the "mother of all," had the greatest temple city in Asia Minor. There were other gods and temples as well (Hestia, Serapis, and Zeus, for example).

Smyrna   There was worship at the temples of Cybele but also Tiberius and Dea Roma. The emperor himself had a temple built in his honor.

Pergamos	In the city of Bishop Polycarp, the martyr, the gods Aesculapius (Asalepios—the god of healing), Athena, Dionysus Serapes, the Egyptian god of the underworld (Re) the Babylonian god Marduk (Bel called Lord) and Zeus were all present.
Thyatira	Tyrimnos, the Lydian sun god, and the gods Borentene and Sambethe were accompanied by their shrines and prophets and prophetess.
Sardis	Sardis had many temples, such as the temple of Zeus Lydius, Men Askenus, Apollo Lycius, Aphrodite Paphia, and Artemis-Persephone.
Philadelphia	Zeus Helios (also called Lydius or Koryphaios) operated as a prosperous religious cult.
Laodicea	The patron was Zeus, father of all gods, as well as the god Men and his temple healing cult.
Rome	The church at Rome was not one of the seven churches mentioned in Revelation, but it was in the capital of the Roman world, with its gods, traditions, and beliefs. Rome started out with gods like Poseidon (god over the sea and ships) but became known for its emperor worship. This set the trend for emperor worship.

Churches must have spiritual effectiveness, prophetic insight, a *rhema* word, and cohesive fellowship. Churches need power in worship and agape relationships.

> None calleth for justice, nor any pleadeth for truth: they trust in vanity, and speak lies; they conceive mischief, and bring forth iniquity. … And judgment is turned away backward, and justice standeth afar off: for truth is fallen in the street, and equity cannot enter. Yea, truth faileth; and he that departeth from evil maketh himself a prey: and the LORD saw it, and it displeased him that there was no justice. (Isaiah 59:4, 14–15)

> For thus hath the Lord said unto me, Go, set a watchman,
> let him declare what he seeth. ... Son of man, I have made
> thee a watchman unto the house of Israel: therefore hear
> the word at my mouth, and give them warning from me.
> (Isaiah 21:6; Ezekiel 3:17)

In regard to the church's role as seer-watchman, one major criticism was that some of the churches in Revelation, including Pergamum and Thyatira, were too permissive of false teaching and teachers. They were guilty of accommodation and compromise. A church that is weak on the inside cannot be strong on the outside.

The churches were guilty of having a weak witnessing record, for the most part. The lamp stands should exercise an insightful role of prophetic witness and a source of shining truth burning in an unbelieving culture and global society. This is, after all, one of the major reasons for the presence and call of the church in the world. "Ye are the light of the world" (Matthew 5:14). The reality of a permeating culture, with its own norms, customs, beliefs, practices, and social pressures, is one of the most difficult realities to see and resist. Culture is a powerful influence and neutralizer of faith and integrity. The effects of culture needed to be addressed in these seven churches. Another important emphasis was upon holding those who teach under subjection. Teachers could not have free reign on matters of spiritual interpretation. Teaching can be used as a means of seduction from sound doctrine and truth. In addition teachers must be aware of the magnitude of alien ideas and practices. Teaching is not the role or niche for false prophets, apostles, and leaders.

The reality of a Christ-centered church was not pervasive and persuasive enough to help turn the tide of an ever-encroaching decadent environment. Later, Islamic culture and religion overtook the entire Asia Minor landscape, through force, trade, and local politics.

Chapter Three

Breaking Out of the Earthly Church to Heavenly Space

In chapter 4 John continues to advance in his spirit state. He beholds and sees more of the heavenly revelation, which will continue throughout the book (Revelation 7:1, 9; 15:5; 18:1; 19:1). The voice of Christ calls John upward into the heavenly realm through the spirit. He (as we are) was able to participate in the transcendence of the spirit world. He sees a throne (mentioned forty-seven times in the book), precious stones, and elders. There are manifestations of lightning, thunder, voices, and seven lamps of fire as the seven spirits of God. There is also the splendor of a sea of crystal-like glass before the throne. Four beasts, or living creatures, full of eyes are around the throne. These creatures represent the highest levels of being and ultimate worship. The four beasts included the wise, majestic eagle, the productive strength of the ox, the ruling might of the lion, and the noble image of the human.

The four living creatures had six wings, reflecting their constant mobility and activeness. They also had many eyes, reflecting their all-seeing character. Nothing could escape their notice. The constant activity, awareness, and praise of the holy one, who was and is and is to come, project the greatness of God. He is always almighty, especially in the midst of darkness and evil in the world. The elders worship him who sits upon the throne and permeates his creation forever. He is worthy and continues to be filled with glory, honor, and power. The creation serves his pleasure and purpose. Human recognition of God includes yielding to his purpose as a way of life. God alone has ultimate intelligence and wise counsel.

Chapter 5 now comes to grip with what is to come and its impact on the world. The world is full of evil and those who do not love justice. The forces of darkness bind those who refuse to repent or change their attitude toward God. He is a universal, cosmic God of love and justice and performs the highest good for his creation.

The time has come to deal with the opening of the mysterious seals that reveal what must come to pass. The problem is, who is worthy to open the book and loose the seals? This is not a matter to be taken lightly; there is much concern about the agent who handles this sacred task. After much weeping by John, one of the elders assures him that there is a Lamb already chosen to open the seven seals. The Lamb, which looked as if it had been slain, had seven horns and seven eyes—the seven spirits of God who roam the earth stood. The Lamb took the book from the right hand of him who sat upon the throne. When this happens, a great moment of worship broke out.

This Lamb of God has a messianic identity. He is special. He is the Lion of the Tribe of Judah, the Root of David. This defines the messianic redeemer, who has come to save us and who now participates in the total plan of God to subdue and recover the entire earthly domain. Every knee must bow and every tongue must confess the sovereignty of the Godhead. The people of the earth must be brought into subjection to the Father and Son. The Kingdom of God must prevail. This hope is embedded in the book of Revelation.

The people of God who have been redeemed by the Lamb serve as kings and priest on the earth. Together, we will overcome with the lamb and reign in place of evil. Many thousands around the throne extol, exalt, lift up, and praise the Lamb, who was sacrificed and who now has power, riches, wisdom, strength, honor, glory, and blessing. In other words, the conquering Christ has every possible resource and attribute needed to accomplish the task. He is the victorious, life-giving power and captain of our salvation. We are with him as a kingdom of ministering priests.

Seven Seals as Justice in Motion

Chapter 6 continues with the transcendent spiritual experience as John hears one of the creatures say, "Come." This marks the beginning of a major set of events. Many scholars think this is where the tribulation begins and continues until chapter 19.

John saw four horses as each seal was opened (Daniel 7:2–8; Zechariah 1:8). The white horse had a rider with a bow and a crown (v. 2). He went forth conquering. The combination of the authorized, legitimate appearance of a white war horse and skilled bow was meant to aim the arrows of judgment and vengeance (Deuteronomy 32:23–26; Ezekiel 5:16–17) for a purposeful mission on the earth. Scholars debate the identity of this horse. Does the horse represent Christ or the evil one, the prince of darkness (Daniel 9:25–27)? The horse seems bent on using his conquering power to gain dominion. His assigned activity is to carry out the will of God, to initiate the wrath of God. The identity of this rider does not seem to fit the Lamb in his role.

The second creature showed him a red horse (v. 4). Power was given to the rider to take peace from the earth. Blood would be shed and humans would kill each other. A great sword would therefore be given. This rider creates conditions that result in the mutual destruction of humankind. Betrayal, deception, seeds of discord, false wisdom, false prophets, false promises, and divisive policies bring about mistrust and strife. Satanic devices serve to weaken any sense of group loyalty, peace, and human community. The use of military might also brings human destruction.

The third creature reveals a black horse (v. 6). A rider sat upon him with a pair of balances in his hand. Famine conditions are at hand. A measure of wheat sold for a day's wages, and three measures of barley for the same amount—many times greater than normal rates. These new famine conditions mean that people will be more obsessed with daily survival than global trends and policies. The voice also stated that the oil and wine should not be hurt but be protected in quality and availability. This is a hint of harsh economic realities, market governance (product control), structured adjustments of commodities, and a command economy. Even the "free market system" is subject to intervention in global society. The presence of global market "managers" may or may not be apparent in worldwide economic institutions. Some scholars believe that the oil and wine (as symbols) are protected as anointed personalities. Goods-based services are subject to pricing and availability controls (13:17).

The fourth seal shows a pale horse, whose rider was called Death and was followed by Hell (v. 8). Both of them were given power over the fourth part of the earth. They had power to kill with the sword, hunger, and death. This is a continuation of the mission of the previous horses in providing an ongoing climate of unrest and turbulence. Fear and disaster are for those who will not repent. They will be pressed beyond measure to submit to God. Nothing will be taken for granted except the sovereignty of the Creator God and his coming reign over heaven and earth. The just will live by faith—in Him. In order to pull off systematic destruction and controls of global resources, attention must be diverted into a worldwide military machine enforcement complex. Other activities will have to suffer.

When the fifth seal is opened, the theme changes to a picture of slain souls under the altar of God (v. 9). These are those who were killed because of the Word of God, who held onto their testimonies. They were waiting for the vengeance of God to occur. They were given white robes and instructed to wait until the time when other martyrs have given their lives for the same cause.

The sixth seal reveals a great earthquake (one of many to come), a blackened sun, and a moon reflecting blood (v. 12). The stars begin to fall, which could represent cosmic stars or significant leading personalities on the earth who were shaken out of their lofty positions due to some episodic chain of events. Public figures and stars can be discredited and discarded. Events and public crises can come as a mighty wind that can cast down figs from its tree before the time. The climatic conditions of the earth are so severe in this seal that nature acts together as a scroll—rolling, folding action shakes everything else out of place. Every level of person, from rulers to indentured servants, will run in panic and paranoia. They will attempt to withdraw from positions of overwhelming danger. They will cry out for certain death as a means to escape the terrible fate of God's wrath. They can't rest between the woes, but they don't repent. So the woes continue. Bible scholars are not certain whether these woes and calamities are in succession or overlap. There appears to be some overlapping; chapters on catastrophic events are interrelated. At the same time we see a series of turbulent activities that lead to both a final clash of good and evil and a final judgment see Isaiah 2:19-21.

John seems to demonstrate that the world cannot continue on its unjust course. This includes man's inhumanity to man and a defiant state of unbelief. In addition, in the process of rejecting God and his mercy, all levels of society must find other forms of messianic or global leadership to sustain their need for security and world stability.

Principalities and Powers Overview

In the past, Bible scholars framed a part of the analysis of Revelation in terms of governments, the governed, and judgments. Governments have fixed, enduring forms and agents to carry out their policies and perspectives. They usually have their own view of society and the generalized public ("the masses"). There are few major roles played by individuals in Revelation. Most of the activities are on a grand scale. National bodies and their representative agents or prophets are used to represent the larger principality, or power. Even the seven churches represent a collective category of evaluated churches held to accountability. Horses that are released for world action represent a collective judgment for the many. The actions in the book of Revelation originate from the kingdom of good or the kingdom of evil.

Governments are personified and represented as collective active bodies, institutions, cities, and nations. The woman, the dragon, the beast, and the horses are all comprehensive concepts. Scholars argue that these collective bodies perform the functions of principalities and powers. They have governmental features. They enact an ideological platform and execute related policies. They can go to war. They can be Antichrist in nature, a global nation-state or corporate institution. They have rules, requirements, and demands they place upon the governed to subdue them. They are driven to make war, oppress, and punish subjects brought under their control. These defacto governments can become ruthless and disregard individual freedoms and ways of thinking.

> And there came out of the smoke locusts upon the earth: and unto them was given power, as the scorpions of the earth have power. (9:3)

And they had a king over them, which is the angel of the bottomless pit, whose name in the Hebrew tongue is Abaddon, but in the Greek tongue hath his name Apollyon. (9:11)

And the dragon was wroth with the woman, and went to make war with the remnant of her seed, which keep the commandments of God, and have the testimony of Jesus Christ. (12:17)

And I stood upon the sand of the sea, and saw a beast rise up out of the sea, having seven heads and ten horns, and upon his horns ten crowns, and upon his heads the name of blasphemy. (13:1)

And I beheld another beast coming up out of the earth; and he had two horns like a lamb, and he spake as a dragon. (13:11)

And the ten horns which thou sawest are ten kings, which have received no kingdom as yet; but receive power as kings one hour with the beast. These have one mind, and shall give their power and strength unto the beast. (17:12–13)

And the woman which thou sawest is that great city, which reigneth over the kings of the earth. (17:18)

There are kings, crowns (6:2), and suffering, with much hunger, thirst, and people without shelter (7:14–16). The more people resist these states, the more they are watched, monitored, punished, or incarcerated. Oppressive governments usually have high prison rates to enforce their unjust policies (Revelation 2:10, Luke 21:12-13). They use an array of methods to bring the population under subjection in order to do the will of the beast. Christ came to take all of this away in due time.

Chapter Four

It's Not Over Yet:
The Seven Seals with More Judgment

As the four horses go forth, we see violent activities among humans, extreme economic conditions, and adversarial living conditions. The second part of chapter 6 deals with natural phenomenon like earthquakes. In chapter 8 we see the destruction and ravishing of the environment as the trumpets sound. In chapters 8, 9, and 16 we see an emphasis upon plagues, disease, and sickness. After these episodes, more emphasis is placed upon beastly activities. All of these events complement the end-time drama that moves toward the ultimate confrontation of good and evil, faith and unbelief, light and darkness, salvation and damnation. The self septet (group of seven) is used in Revelation to reflect a complete picture of all aspects of unresolved conflict, fierce competition for resources, and widespread deception.

In contrast to the unjust kingdoms of this world is the just Kingdom of our Lord. Both involve governments, rulers, and belief systems.

> And round about the throne were four and twenty seats: and upon the seats I saw four and twenty elders sitting, clothed in white raiment; and they had on their heads crowns of gold. (4:4)

> The four and twenty elders fall down before him that sat on the throne, and worship him that liveth for ever and ever, and cast their crowns before the throne ... (4:10)

And the rest of the men which were not killed by these plagues yet repented not of the works of their hands, that they should not worship devils, and idols of gold, and silver, and brass, and stone, and of wood: which neither can see, nor hear, nor walk: Neither repented they of their murders, nor of their sorceries, nor of their fornication, nor of their thefts. (9:20–21)

And the voice which I heard from heaven spake unto me again, and said, Go and take the little book which is open in the hand of the angel which standeth upon the sea and upon the earth. And I went unto the angel, and said unto him, Give me the little book. And he said unto me, Take it, and eat it up; and it shall make thy belly bitter, but it shall be in thy mouth sweet as honey. And I took the little book out of the angel's hand, and ate it up; and it was in my mouth sweet as honey: and as soon as I had eaten it, my belly was bitter. And he said unto me, Thou must prophesy again before many peoples, and nations, and tongues, and kings. (10:8–11).

God is represented by his throne (4:2; 20:4). In the final clash between good and evil, the Lord seizes the kingdom of this world (11:15–18). Many scholars assert that the battle of Armageddon (19:14–21) is fought with collective governments coming together. The fight is about credibility and dominion. After Christ has put down all rule and authority, unjust governments will be replaced by Christ-centric rule. He will reign a "thousand years" (20:4, 6). This is called the millennium, Christ's rule on earth. Christ and his saints, the bride as the church, shall come together at the marriage supper of the Lamb. Here, the first resurrection of the just occurs. (See the discussion later.) Paradise in the New Jerusalem implies the re-creation of a new life space, since there will have been mass destruction and pollution on the old earth (21:1–2). A new earth will be necessary with a new heaven. There are debates about the location and its constituents. Who will be in heaven or on the earth before, during, and after the millennium, and what about the two resurrections? These matters are subject to much discussion. (The discussions are included in each related section of this book, *Revelation Now*, as they arise in the apocalypse (John's book) itself.

In the meantime, God's witnesses must see and perform what is good and what the Lord requires of us—to do justly and to love mercy and to walk humbly with God (Micah 6:8). God continues to work to draw people unto himself in many ways in the end-time age to act out His will. People of the world are expected to respond in faith and submission when the prophet-servants of God warn them. Much of the book of the Revelation of John is aimed or purposed to alert, inform and persuade the masses to turn to God. Shall a trumpet be blown in the city, and the people not be afraid? shall there be evil in a city, and the Lord hath not done it? ... The lion hath roared, who will not fear? the Lord God hath spoken, who can but prophesy? ... For they know not to do right, saith the LORD, who store up violence and robbery in their palaces (Amos 3:6, 8, 10).

The Tributes and Tribulation Survivors

Chapter 7 begins with an interlude, a break from the vision of coming violence, famine, and death. In this section four angels stand guard on the four corners or ends of the earth. Their assignment is to prevent the four winds from hurting the earth, sea, or trees. Some reference can be made to Zechariah's (6:5) four horses and the winds of Jeremiah's destructive chariots and horses (4:11–13, 49:36). Jeremiah lived under the rule of Assyria, Egypt, and Babylon. (Note again the historic empire background of God's intervention.) King Nebuchadnezzar of Babylon acted as the lion destroyer of Jerusalem.

An angel arises from the east with the seal of God (Ezekiel 9:34). This angel instructs the four previous angels who control the four winds not to hurt the earth, sea, or trees before the servants of God have been sealed in their foreheads (Revelation 9:3). In other words, they are to provide a safe environment for the servants of God. Some interpret this act as protection for the church from judgmental winds or the forces of evil during some eschatological period. God's people usually appeal to God for protection and intervention in a major crisis. For example, in 2 Kings 19:4, 9, and 16, Hezekiah petitioned

God to deliver Israel from King Sennacherib of Assyria as well as the intimidation of Tirhakah, king of Ethiopia.

The number to be sealed were 144,000, and they were to come from each of the tribes of Israel (except Dan, the tribe associated with idolatry). Each of the twelve tribes had 12,000 sealed. There is much speculation, but it is not known what the full significance of this identity and number means for Israel or the church. By this time the twelve tribes of Israel ceased to exist. The reader can explore this significance for his own enlightenment. The messianic tribe of Judah is, however, mentioned first. The chosen are sealed or affirmed and marked for divine security through the presence of the Holy Spirit.

The second number to be announced included a number that no one could count. This multitude of persons from all nations (ethnic groups) and people, including different languages or dialects, emphasizes the complete universality of God. God is no respecter of persons (Acts 10:34).

> Neither is worshiped with men's hands, as though he needed any thing, seeing he giveth to all life, and breath, and all things; And hath made of one blood all nations of men for to dwell on all the face of the earth, and hath determined the times before appointed, and the bounds of their habitation; That they should seek the Lord, if haply they might feel after him, and find him, though he be not far from every one of us. (Acts 17:25–27)

This unnumbered multitude stood in their white robes with palms in their hands worshiping the one who sat upon the throne and the Lamb. The angels, the elders, and the four living creatures all fell before the throne in worship. One of the elders identified this multitude as the group who came out of great tribulation and had washed their robes and made them white in the blood of the Lamb (Revelation 7:14). This blood had a powerful atoning effect on removing the sins of those who believed and repented. It was an act of perfecting the spirit of believers, who were not perfect (Hebrews 12:23, 26, 27).

> How much more shall the blood of Christ, who through the eternal Spirit offered himself without spot to God, purge your conscience from dead works to serve the living

God? ... And almost all things are by the law purged with blood; and without shedding of blood is no remission. ... For then must he often have suffered since the foundation of the world: but now once in the end of the world hath he appeared to put away sin by the sacrifice of himself. (Hebrews 9:14, 22, 26)

Those who have been redeemed now serve God day and night before the throne, as God dwells among them. Through the one who sits upon the throne and the Lamb, all suffering of any kind will be eliminated as they dwell in the midst of the fountain of living waters. Believers can now serve day and night in his temple. No hunger, thirst, overexposure to blistering pressure, heat of conflict, stress, or adversarial conditions will distract them from a life of honoring God completely. These are they who did not lose confidence, faith, and inner peace. They did not become psychotic, stressed out, erratic, unstable, or shaken in mind (2 Thessalonians 2:2; Luke 21:25) They did not panic, fear, or flee. They were stable.

Time Interludes In and Beyond History

John declares that he has seen, heard, and experienced the presence, the hand of Christ, the events to come. He has wept, worshiped, and rejoiced. In Revelation, John refers often to different dimensions of time. His narrative is both in and beyond history. Related terms include:

> Beginning and the end
> Forever and ever
> Is, was, and is to come
> Hereafter, quickly, soon, shortly
> Ten days
> Time and times and a half
> Forty and two months
> A thousand two hundred and three score days
> One thousand years
> One hour

Refer to Revelation 1:1, 8, 10, 3:3, 11:29, 13, 12:12, 14, 18:17, 20:3, 5, 22:20

Narrative time in Revelation is mixed with historic and eternal time between heaven, earth, and the abyss. The Spirit was and is speaking to the churches. John sees, hears, and experiences that which is and is to come. Occurrences involving turbulence, plagues, and prayers are dispersed in time. References to the plagues of Egypt and the visions of Daniel and Zechariah represent both flashbacks and future images and impact. There are mixed tenses and long delays, which include a lot of action after John says "things which must shortly come to pass." Dealing with a time frame with overlapping events like plagues and tribulation (6:2, 4–8; 8:7–8; 9:3, 14; 15:1) is a very elusive endeavor. Yet, there are connections to observed phenomenon in time and global context. So we watch, worship, and pray. We yield to the will of God in our circumstances. As God takes his "time" in the spiraling themes and events, the time line remains coherent.

There is an eschatological and theological order in this spiral of events— those ideas, concepts, and events that are repeated with new variations and deeper meaning. There are differences in degree and scale as time and history unfold. Even the same phrases might have a different meaning in time, place, and circumstances. This is why we need ongoing guidance and interpretation through the Holy Spirit (John 14:26; 16:13; Revelation 1:10–11). In the ancient style of writing, related ideas may be inserted in the discourse before returning to the main theme or motif. This is true of some epistles and in the writing of St. Augustine (AD 354–430).

Trumpet Visions Continue

In chapter 8 John returns to address the systematic opening of the seals after the seventh seal was opened. The trumpet visions return to elaborate on future conditions. This was preceded by an impacting one-half hour of meditative silence.

After this seven angels who stood before God were given seven trumpets. Another angel came before the altar and was given much incense to be offered with the prayers of all saints upon the golden altar before the throne. No trumpet is blown before prayer activity has occurred. John reported that the smoke of the incense with the prayers ascended up before God out of the angels' hands. The censer was subsequently filled with fire and thrown to the earth, accompanied with voices, thunder, lightning, and an earthquake. This act of receiving the prayers was met with a serious response from God, as attested by a reaction of the earthy elements.

The first angel sounded a trumpet, followed by hail and fire mixed with blood (v. 7). This mixture, when cast to the earth, burned one third of the trees and all green grass. The second angel sounded and a mountain of fire was cast into the sea, and one third of the sea became blood (v. 8). One third of the sea life (marine life) and ships were destroyed. These two trumpets involve the destruction of forestry (fires), sea contamination, and discoloration (like one of the plagues in Egypt). These environmental tragedies affect select parts of the earth and make life unbearable. No matter where the specific areas of calamities are, the whole earth and people are in some way affected by these acute events. Even news of these events can be disheartening. When ecological systems are out of balance due to calamities, war, and misuse and abuse of the environment, there is an acceleration of environmental degeneration. The quality of food decreases. Both human and animal immune systems are weakened. Sickness, disease and plagues experience major increases (Garrett, Laurie).

The third angel sounded, and a great star from heaven, burning brightly, fell upon a third part of the rivers and waters (v. 10). A third of the waters became bitter, which meant death for many, because of the star Wormwood that fell into them.

After the fourth sounded, one third of the sun, moon, and stars was darkened (v. 12). A third part of the day and night had a blockage of light. An angel flying in the sky warned that there was more woe to come.

The sounding angels with trumpets continued to sound in chapter 9. The fifth trumpet showed a falling star from heaven who was a personality to whom was given the key to the bottomless pit (v. 1). When he opened the pit, great smoke came out and darkened the sun and the air. Again, there is great environmental pollution released, which began to affect the health and well-being of people. The locusts came out of the smoke as a pollutant with scorpion power. In fact, they had to be restricted in their damage. They were told not to hurt the grass, greenery, or trees but were allowed to inflict godless people, who did not have the seal of God and refused to repent (v. 20). The implication of protecting greenery increases the likelihood of international competition for land that produces vegetation in the world. Under such adverse climatic conditions good land would become scarce (8:7). The agents of adversity were instructed to torment unsealed persons for five months but not to kill them. It is amazing that unbelievers fought so hard in their (hardened) hearts against God. These also included demon and idol worshipers. (Worship is a major theme in Revelation. It is an important centering act in recognizing ultimate authority, sovereignty, and honor.)

This passage reminds us of the verses in chapter 6 that refer to environmental hurt, human misery, and torment, both natural and human in origin. The fallen stars observed in 6:1–3 causing fear, torment, and panic seem to be a part of a continuous episode of disintegrating powers or collective personalities of evil.

> And all the host of heaven shall be dissolved, and the heavens shall be rolled together as a scroll: and all their host shall fall down, as the leaf falleth off from the vine, and as a falling fig from the fig tree. (Isaiah 34:4)

Chapter 9 continues with locust advancing as men and horses prepared for battle, a familiar theme. These horses act as organized forces to inflict pain and discomfort. The locusts had tails with stings, like those of scorpions.

A locust's life span is five months. In the Bible, five is symbolic of selected but partial examples of a truth. There were five foolish virgins, five illegal husbands in John, five talents, five yoke of oxen, five brothers of the rich man, five loaves of bread, and five sparrows that are not forgotten by God in Luke, Matthew 16:9, 25:1, 15, Luke 12:6, 14:19, 16:28, John 4:18. All that God is looking for in this passage is for people who will recognize and confess Christ before the world. The same Christ will confess them before the angels of God (Luke 12:5–9). There is no need to fear those who kill the body, but to fear the one who has the power to cast into hell.

The account in chapter 9 reports that there was a locust king, the angel of the bottomless pit. His name is *Abaddon* ("destruction") in

Hebrew and *Apollyon* ("destroyer") in Greek. The sixth angel was given orders to sound and loose the four bound angels at the river Euphrates (Genesis 2:14; 15:18 Deuteronomy 1:7; Revelation 16:12). These released angels prepared for the hour, month, and day to slay one third of humanity. Many thousands of horsemen, as a great army, were used in this assignment. These horses with lion heads destroyed people by fire, smoke, and brimstone. The horsemen, or riders, had power in their tongues/mouths and in their tails as evil (demonic) influence. Some interpret the tails as weaponry of a military vehicle. The after effect of plagues led to more serpent-like mindsets and false, deceptive wisdom spoken among unbelievers. This was the first of three woes to come. The woes were intermixed with the calamities of the seven sounding angels.

Those exposed to these calamities continue in their mundane ways of materialism, false gods, greed, and devil worship. They continue to engage in murder, sorcery, spiritual fornication, theft, and manufactured public consent. That is they allow themselves to be influenced by the false teachings and ideology of the beast who creates his own line of thinking and perpetuates his ideas as a public companion.

The chapter ends by saying that these persons didn't even look back or reflect on these dreadful conditions. They did not repent. They instead rebelled against God. Some scholars believe this intense period represents the first half of the tribulation period. The problem is not merely repentance but acceptance. The messianic identity of Jesus as the saving Lamb of God must be accepted. Jesus Christ as Lord (*Kyrios*) must define and direct the life of the believing, receiving person. This also implies a rejection of competing norms, defied personalities, and mundane beliefs that stand in opposition to the living God-Word. Acceptance of the Lord God means agreement with all that God is and compatibility with his Holy Spirit. It is not practice versus belief but practice *and* belief. It is the holistic acceptance of the Kingdom of God, life, and principles. These principles are the mind-thoughts of God acted out. They are not a rigid, legal system of proper practices but the absorption of the leading, revealing Spirit of God without resistance. They are a natural outcome of a spiritual relationship, the consequence of a mutual love affair between the Creator and the creature.

Responding to Catastrophes: Disaster Economics

There are questions about institutional response to catastrophic consequences and sorrows present during the time (Matthew 24:8). Will global authorities come to the aid of the intended or unintended victims? Is there a practice of protecting select commodities? Are there off-limit categories of wrath? Each ruler seeks to protect the interest of his own servants. Obviously, there is some deliberate plan or policy that excludes or includes some kind of protection, rescue, covering, or exemption for those who either serve the beast or resist the beast and serve God. In fact, one purpose of imposing the mark of the beast is to delineate or structure preference. This is a means of social-political stratification.

There are two marks: one mark is of the beast and the other, the mark of God (9:4; 13:17). Apparently, agents of the beast and agents of God will be working out the purpose of the two powers. God will be active, even during the tribulation, when it seems that he is absent. He still cares and has ways yet to be understood to comfort his own people. At the same time, ways of protecting and subsidizing the ruling elite and their welfare will be in place to maintain those loyal to the beast. In other words the purpose of creating a system of categorizing "marking" or identifying the population is to reward, approve or disapprove who is to receive goods, services and employment. Those who are global administrators will oversee this process. Somebody has to do it.

During times of earthquakes, wars, plagues, pestilences, and counter-violence, everyone will be affected. In fact, the powers of this world including religious orders promote division, civil unrest, and terrorism. *"Emergency"* policies are created that will include disaster economics that favor some and complicate help for others. Loyal subjects gain quick access to aid and questionable ones are closely regulated. For instance, Rome offered to help rebuild the city and to assist earthquake disaster victims in Laodicea, during the earthquake years of A.D. 60 – 100, a city loyal to the emperor. Disaster economics is a powerful, selective weapon to carry out empire strategies and agenda. The beast has his own monetary fund for wars, punishment, and reward. These funds are made available to struggling nations that eventually will collapse. The waiting beast absorbs struggling nations within its domain through conditional assistance, severe terms of support, or outright annexation and hostile takeovers. Sometimes having access to certain technology and schools like the Laodicean medical school requires allegiance to related cults and belief systems. In the case of Laodicea assistance from Rome was politely turned down.

Chapter Five

Another Break: Interlude of Reflection

Chapter 10 deals with another interlude because the seventh angel does not sound the trumpet until 11:15. At this sounding, great voices declare that the "kingdoms of this world are become the kingdoms of our Lord, and of his Christ; and he shall reign for ever and ever."

The use of the plural for the "kingdoms of this world" seems to imply that the goal of the beast to completely unify the world under his authority never occurs. As we shall see, there is great success in bringing the kings into a type of beastly compliance. The kings align themselves in some kind of ideological and military alliance. Some smaller nation-states may come together to create a stronger base against larger mega structures (with varying success), but there are still distinct nation-states, territories, or unions that exist and have the designation of "kingdom" with perhaps strong connections between them.

The problem with demonic unity is that it is the nature of evil to be suspicious of everyone, to encourage mistrust that spills over to mistrusting the leader, no matter who he is. Evil can never be free of doubt, conflict, tension, selfishness, and pride. Its innate nature is flawed and divisive. A sense of unity can be manufactured and coerced by ideology, false values, and instigated fear, but it doesn't last. The inner impulse of ungodly life is toward disintegration and self-aggrandizement. No worldly covenant, agreement, or treaty is safe from change, revoking, or total disregard. In fact, agreements can be acknowledgments of mistrust because they imply some kind of bound equalization and that recognition must be imposed upon the other as a restraint on one or all of the parties involved. Some may seek complete independence and sovereignty above anyone, God withstanding. This is why the willingness to agree to repent and submit to God is such a major challenge.

Take note that John interweaves all of this unrepentance and human rebellion with several accounts of believer's submission and worship. God's people honor the Creator.

> And the four and twenty elders, which sat before God on their seats, fell upon their faces, and worshiped God, Saying, We give thee thanks, O Lord God Almighty, which art, and wast, and art to come; because thou hast taken to thee thy great power, and hast reigned. (Revelation 11:16–17)

Also note that in 11:18 the nations were angry. They did not want to face God, deal with God, or be judged by God most of all. But the saints will be rewarded for steadfast faith and fear of God. Yes, after all that suffering, pain, and earthly rejection, God rewards his people. Servants, the prophets, and saints that fear his name will be given authority over the destroyers. So it is no wonder that Psalm 2:1 in colloquial language asks:

"What in the world is the heathen raving about? What are the people imagining?" Are they upset because they realize their ability to perpetuate their vanity will not last?

> Why do the heathen [nations] rage, and the people imagine a vain thing? The kings of the earth set themselves, and the rulers take counsel together, against the LORD, and against his anointed, saying, Let us break their bands asunder, and cast away their cords from us. He that sitteth in the heavens shall laugh: the LORD shall have them in derision. ... Be wise now therefore, O ye kings: be instructed, ye judges of the earth. Serve the LORD with fear, and rejoice with trembling. Kiss the Son, lest he be angry, and ye perish from the way, when his wrath is kindled but a little. Blessed are all they that put their trust in him. (Psalm 2:1–4, 10–12)

Now that we have dealt with all of the trumpets in chapters 8, 9, and a part of 11, we can proceed to deal with the interlude from chapters 10—12.

Chapter 10 is mostly about the little book of prophesy. From an earthly position John sees the mighty angel coming down from heaven in a chariot cloud with the reflection of a rainbow in his hand and his face as the sun. His feet were as pillars of fire—the burning presence of God. As the angel approaches, John can see that he has an open book (Revelation) in his hand. His right foot is upon the sea and his left foot is on the land, symbolizing his authority and dominion over both. The angel cries with a thunderous voice, "Seal up those things which the seven thunders uttered, and write them not" (v. 4). The angel looks up to heaven and swears (vows). He declares that in the days (time period or season) when the seventh angel begins to sound, the mystery and message of God will finally be unfolded and completed. There will be a full manifestation that will bring together a full perspective and the plan of God for humanity. This will include the acts of God through the law, grace, and prophetic judgments upon unbelievers and the nations of this world.

John then responds to the request of the angel to come and take the open book now being made available to him. The angel instructs him to eat the little book, which is as sweet as honey yet produces bitterness in the belly. The news from God is good until deeper reflection and digestion produces a bitterness within. The prophet who eats senses the goodness of God and also the bitter rejection of the people. Many who initially hear the news soon realize it requires total surrender and repentance. They must make choices to renounce the gods of this world for messianic love and kindness. John is reminded that his assignment and call to prophesy on an international basis is not yet completed.

The Two Witnesses

Chapter 11 is the second part of this three-part interval. This part deals mainly with the account of the two anointed witnesses, olive trees called candlesticks in verse 4. First, John is told to measure the temple of God, the altar, and those who worship there (v. 1). John is asked to engage in some kind of assessment of the temple of God, the heavenly city—Jerusalem, or the Christian church in general. The outer court could represent true believers. These are also those who have been persecuted. In the New Testament, *temple* often refers to the church of Christ, the people of God. These believers have been "measured" or set aside for God's spiritual covering.

Verse 3 says the gentiles will be given a limited, defined period of influence over the church to carry out destructive or hindering activities. This period will be forty-two months (Daniel 7:25; 12:7; Revelation 12:14; 13:5). This period is equal to what is called "a time, and times, and half a time," or forty-two months, or 1,260 days.

Generally the two witnesses called olive trees are regarded as two anointed servants of God (Zechariah 4;11-12). They are reminders of God's message that the work of motivation and the empowerment of his people will continue through the spirit of God not the might and power of human agents. These anointed witnesses will have credibility in direct contrast to deceivers, false teachers and false prophecy.

The writer goes on to describe the role of the two witnesses. Some scholars believe they represent part of the faithful church. They are to be protected. They can stop the rain from heaven during their prophecy and unleash plagues or disease at will. Only when their mission is finished will the beast, or representative from the evil, bottomless pit (the abyss), be able to assassinate them. Their bodies will lie in the street three and a half days in a place called Egypt and Sodom. These are also places of the crucifixion of Christ. Egypt represents the oppressor nation, and Sodom represents the abundance of corrupt wisdom and practices as the norm. Both were over turned by the overcoming power of God. The crucifixion of Christ occurs wherever the conspiracy of evil is at work to undermine the legitimacy of Christ and the messianic mission. The place is a product of the event. In other words, evil practices create evil environments.

After the three and a half days have passed and people have rejoiced over their unburied bodies, God steps in. People are tormented by truth, and God is truth. God puts his life-giving spirit within the witnesses. They stand on their feet and are called by God into heaven before their foes. At the same time, a great earthquake kills a tenth of the city, and the survivors give glory to the Lord in fear. The account of persecution of the two witnesses is called the second woe. The third woe is said to be coming quickly in the scenes to follow.

Following this episode, the seventh angel sounds: "The kingdoms of this world are becoming the kingdoms of our Lord, and of his Christ; and he shall reign for ever and ever." Immediately worship breaks out in heaven and the temple of God. The victory cry is made against the destructive foes.

> I saw in the night visions, and, behold, one like the Son of man came with the clouds of heaven, and came to the Ancient of days, and they brought him near before him. And there was given him dominion, and glory, and a kingdom, that all people, nations, and languages, should serve him: his dominion is an everlasting dominion, which shall not pass away, and his kingdom that which shall not be destroyed. (Daniel 7:13–14)

The Persecuted Woman and Child: Prehistory and Human History

The last part of the three part interlude culminates in chapter 12. This chapter is about the woman with child who is under attack by the great red dragon with seven heads, ten horns, and seven crowns upon his head. This is the dragon whose tail brought down a third of the rebellious angels who were cast out of heaven. Michael and his angels defeated the dragon, who is also called the accuser, the serpent, the devil, and Satan. It was primarily the blood of the Lamb, the Word, and the cross that overcame indictments against humanity (Colossians 2:14–15).

> That thou shalt take up this proverb against the king of Babylon, and say, How hath the oppressor ceased! the golden city ceased! The LORD hath broken the staff of the wicked, and the sceptre of the rulers. … How art thou fallen from heaven, O Lucifer, son of the morning! how art thou cut down to the ground, which didst weaken the nations! For thou hast said in thine heart, I will ascend

into heaven, I will exalt my throne above the stars of God: I will sit also upon the mount of the congregation, in the sides of the north: I will ascend above the heights of the clouds; I will be like the most High. Yet thou shalt be brought down to hell, to the sides of the pit. They that see thee shall narrowly look upon thee, and consider thee, saying, Is this the man that made the earth to tremble, that did shake kingdoms; That made the world as a wilderness, and destroyed the cities thereof; that opened not the house of his prisoners? (Isaiah 14:4–5, 12–17)

And the seventy returned again with joy, saying, Lord, even the devils are subject unto us through thy name. And he said unto them, I beheld Satan as lightning fall from heaven. Behold, I give unto you power to tread on serpents and scorpions, and over all the power of the enemy: and nothing shall by any means hurt you. (Luke 10:17–19)

Thereafter, the woman who bore the man-child, the church, and the saints all came under attack. The woman had to escape to the wilderness (Egypt) and hid from the serpent-dragon who was enraged. She hid for 1,260 days, protected and fed by God. Again, this period was also called a "time and times and the dividing of time" (Daniel 7:20–22, 25). No matter what flood of adversity was thrust upon the woman, God was able to swallow up and eliminate the flood.

Chapter Six

How the Dragon Pulls It Off: Global Rule and Beastly Agenda

Chapter 13 is a major chapter in the book of Revelation. It has two main parts to it. The first part highlights the beast who rises from the sea in John's vision. The beast rises from the vast mystery and depth of the sea, imitating the logos-mind substance coming out of eternity into earthly time as the ruling principle of life. Christ emerged from the Godhead into human life-space and history. The cosmic sea monster has seven heads and ten horns (the ruling Roman Empire). Each of the ten horns has ten crowns. Upon the heads the name *blasphemy* is written. Each head represents a power center or regional authority. The ten horns also represent inflated arrogance beyond real, ultimate power. The projection of ten horns makes a symbolic statement in that seven represents completeness. This is an act of self-deification and false sovereignty. The beast wares a royal diadem on his head.

The sea beast is the ultimate source and guarantor of the will, power, and mind-set of evil. He is like a leopard, with feet like a bear and a mouth like a lion (v. 2). The beast acts quickly; he is forceful (mighty) and vicious. He is a combination of many things. He is well-structured to carry out his international work. (In the Old Testament world the female beast called Leviathan represented universal evil, chaos, and the unknown darkness of the deep.) see Psalm 74:13-14, Psalm 104:26, Isaiah 27:1, 51:9, Daniel 7:3, Amos 9:3. The monster or dragon was also used as a military ensign by the Roman army. The dragon gave the beast his power and seat of great authority. This seat (office, throne) implies some kind of institutional or governmental position, authority, and rule. The term *beast* refers to a hostile ruler, a tyrannical monarch or government. The beast has both a political and theological mind. He has a strategy of networking, persuasion, indoctrination, and rational discourse designed to justify and perpetuate his influence and administrative reign. He is intelligent and clever.

One of the heads of the beast appeared to be wounded unto death (v. 3). However, by some miracle-like action the beast was revived, cured, or raised up again. This restoration of the wounded beast prompts a global response of worship and adoration directed toward the dragon, who empowered the beast. No one is recognized as equal to the beast in war, greatness, divinity, or in speech. The bold beast spoke slander and blasphemy against God and his tabernacle (church) for forty-two months, or 1,260 days.

The same period of three and a half years was used under King Antiochus IV Epiphanes of Greece to desecrate the temple and also under Titus of Rome to destroy the second temple in AD 70. Antiochus wanted to turn the temple into a temple to worship Zeus (175–164 BCE). He had a pig placed upon the altar for sacrifice. Judah Maccabee and the Maccabees revolted later. Hanukkah, a rededication celebration, was instituted. Some scholars believe that the book of Daniel (520 BCE) was written by more than one author around the time of Antiochus IV, the little horn (187–175 BCE). The theme of Daniel is very similar to Revelation in that the emphasis is on the controlling, revealing, sovereignty of God in history, in the context of historic empires.

In chapter 13 the beast is given a specific length of time to enact any decrees. All believers of the earth who had no saving knowledge of God (whose names were not written in the book of life) eventually become active worshipers of the beast. The beast immediately uses his authority to make war with (persecute) the saints and rule over global affairs and people for a while. The patience and faith of the saints is challenged under deliberate oppression. The beast determines who will live or die, receive support, privileges of food, health provisions, nourishment, and more (Revelation 6:8; 13:15–16; Hebrews 2:14–15).

The cosmic sea monster appears to be the origin, center, or mastermind of evil. Evil imagination and international turbulence is designed to lead to a new justified order of structured social-political life. It will take on the form of a dominating kingdom of evil in the world. This kingdom might first appear to be benevolent before it becomes fully confident and established. It operates through connecting institutions, ideology, and authority. In other words, the dragon works to enact a global system for its agenda. We have already seen in chapter 6 that this system affects the economic (including wages) and political realms of world society (6:15). Food distribution, bonuses, and credit worthiness could be determined by a FICA-type score (factor reading) as manifested in the mark of the beast (13:16–18). All operations will assume an institutional form in order to execute this worldwide plan effectively.

It's possible that the sea beast will be responsible for rearranging the political map of the world into special regions and territories. This female beast called Leviathan in Hebrew literature (Job 41:1) brings her chaos into the social structures of the world. Rule in these territories will be parceled out. Supervision will be a centered approach because of the global network that connects all of these regions to one mind and one international apparatus. This process will change how the world communicates. In other words, the beast will control the information flow. The decline of nation-states represents an opportunity for future re-territorialization and control. This leads to tighter global governance. An operation of this size will, of course, have many weaknesses, failures, and setbacks. But the intent remains the same. The benevolent beast, who appears like a lamb, comes to rule over the docile sheep of the world. In Matthew 7:16 Jesus warns his disciples about false prophets who come as wolves in sheep's clothing. The beast will resist any form of negotiation or power sharing. He resents all "outside" organizations. In this regard, social control and religion become major matters because they represent potential areas of independence.

The second beast, or land beast or false prophet/leader, has two horns like a lamb and designated authority (vv. 11–12). This beast in the Old Testament or Hebrew tradition was called the male behemoth. He is the *Ogdoas* or *Sophia*, verse 13:18 the intelligent beast can only be understood through the wisdom that he has clothed himself in. He is a puzzle to unravel in the Greek Gnostic system. (Job 40:15, 4 Ezra 6:47-54, and Enoch 60:7-8 as outside sources also see J. M. Ford, Revelation). He is able to perform some feats that evoke public admiration. This beast appears to be the communications and educational arm of the sea beast. He speaks false wisdom like the dragon, and his task is to confuse, cause doubt, and seduce people away from the truth. The land beast seems to operate on a more personal, localized, and ideological level. He permeates local spaces and places with doctrinal ideas, worship, and manufactured consent. He is the "public relations agent" and disseminator of misinformation. The beast can create a group mind-set to help alleviate the felt pain of the people. As a lamb-looking beast, his job is to solidify, spy, and decry. He wants to be seen as benevolent and yet strong.

The Lamb is mentioned twenty-six times in Revelation. Worship is mentioned about twenty-four times. Therefore, these are very important creature-concepts. The Leviathan Beast (Job 41:1-15) steals the Lamb label but does not have the Lamb character/nature. He rewrites and teaches distorted history to support his own worldview. He "gives life" by making the image of the beast a reality in the daily lives of people. The beast credentializes and approves various personalities and roles. He counterfeits labels, but the true essence is replaced. This means that the beast takes upon himself the label of benevolent, honorable ruler when he in fact is a deceiver and the lawless one. He comes as an angel of light but his agenda is to make war. (2 Thessalonians 2:4, 8-9; 2 Peter 2:10-12) He can slander or endorse. (2 Corinthians 11:13-14) He stamps his mark of approval on the forehead or right hand of the population. The beast himself has a computerized number of 666, from numbers added within his name. (In ancient times each letter of a name was assigned a value; thus, the beast's number comes from numbers added within his name.)

The beast is a master at the practical application of beastly theology, or false religion. He masters the process of systemic evil. Infrastructures are built and supervised by the land beast. This includes devising a system to mark or identify every living person in order to monitor their allegiances, practices, and personal persuasions. Sophisticated tracking methods will need to be put in place in order to enact global population control. Allocation of world resources will be preplanned. The beastly system will require extensive administrative centers and personnel. And until the Lord comes, the beast will be obsessed with himself.

The purpose of the true messianic Lamb is to feed and lead into worship, cleanse believers, open seals, and carry out the wrath of God. In the process the Lamb will also establish God's kingdom on earth. He is first and last! The false prophet/lamb-looking beast creates a false priesthood to intercept true, godly believers. But truth wins over deceit. The beast can never become divine. His priests are not anointed. The "do it yourself" distorted gospel will remain empty and powerless. God alone appoints his priest to his universal priesthood ministry (Revelation 1:5–6, 5:9–10).

The beast's government and network will make great pronouncements, edicts, rules, and legislation. These edicts will work together to control all social, educational, and political life in the city-states of the world. National boundaries will have little significance. The beast will have easy access to all international markets and military units whenever necessary. He will be able to make war or to engage in forceful, hostile, aggressive actions with or without military weapons. He will apply much pressure on saints in particular to gain full submission. Resistance to the beast deprives him of the recognition and glory he craves.

The land beast also has the role of creating a new world order theology. He will draw on all theologies to win over followers with minimum resistance. The theology will point to and reinforce his status as world leader and spiritual-political "messiah."

> Let no man deceive you by any means: for that day shall not come, except there come a falling away first, and that man of sin be revealed, the son of perdition; Who opposeth and exalteth himself above all that is called God, or that is worshiped; so that he as God sitteth in the temple of God, shewing himself that he is God. … And then shall that Wicked be revealed, whom the Lord shall consume with the spirit of his mouth, and shall destroy with the brightness of his coming: Even him, whose coming is after the working of Satan with all power and

signs and lying wonders, And with all deceivableness of unrighteousness in them that perish; because they received not the love of the truth, that they might be saved. And for this cause God shall send them strong delusion, that they should believe a lie: That they all might be damned who believed not the truth, but had pleasure in unrighteousness. (2 Thessalonians 2:3–4, 8–12)

Take note, however, that the wicked one still works under some restrictions until the time comes for his full exposure and removal.

The world leader and/or the oligarchy (a small ruling elite) will supplant laws by becoming the law. They become lawless by recreating the law. New codes of behavior, deviance, and compliance will be instituted. The lawless one who operates above law will appear to be a person of the law, yet he knows no law beyond himself. The law he imposes will legitimize his role, actions, and identity. These "laws" will actually be distortions of true law. Law will be used as a tool for unrighteous motives and practices. They will reflect beastly theology and help to direct worship and respect to the dragon. The law will coordinate governance, compliance, and public thinking. The worldview and spin of the beast will be disguised in the law.

Laws reflect those who make law. The lawless one uses the common respect for law to implement unjust law. His law will be used to circumvent just and divine law. The beast will determine what a crime is and what the punishment is (13:15). This can be called law and (new) order. The beast exercises legal control to restrict freedom. He uses statutes and regulations and exacting procedures to entangle people and their activities. He is obsessed with monitoring, labeling, and validating the population. The lawlessness of a chaotic social-political order will create ideal circumstances for the false leader to rescue the fearful ones who want to avoid a total sense of lostness and despair. Therefore, the beast comes as law-giver and leader. As Moses brought the law and Jesus brought divine teaching, so does the beast bring his "enlightened" message.

Who changed the truth of God into a lie, and worshipped and served the creature more than the Creator, who is blessed for ever. Amen. (Romans 1:25)

For it is written, I will destroy the wisdom of the wise, and will bring to nothing the understanding of the prudent. Where is the wise? where is the scribe? where is the disputer of this world? hath not God made foolish the wisdom of this world? (1 Corinthians 1:19–20)

Notwithstanding I have a few things against thee, because thou sufferest that woman Jezebel, which calleth herself a prophetess, to teach and to seduce my servants to commit fornication, and to eat things sacrificed unto idols. (Revelation 2:20)

And there followed another angel, saying, Babylon is fallen, is fallen, that great city, because she made all nations drink of the wine of the wrath of her fornication. (Revelation 14:8)

And the light of a candle shall shine no more at all in thee; and the voice of the bridegroom and of the bride shall be heard no more at all in thee: for thy merchants were the great men of the earth; for by thy sorceries were all nations deceived. (Revelation 18:23)

The distortion of law is one more reason why the Word of God as truth is important. People will have little means to gauge legitimacy or authorize values and justice without the Word and the Spirit. What is good taste or bad practice will be difficult to measure in the new order of things. The widespread use of the word **deception** *in Revelation as well as in Matthew 24:11, 2 Thessalonians 2:9-10 and 2 Timothy 3:13* implies the fallacy of human thinking. A new world logic will be put in place. This logic is a part of the cosmic scheme of false thinking. There will be new kinds of inequity and stratification and new policies concerning the distribution of goods and services. There will be self-perpetuating policies and role assignments put in place. The Beast will determine who is worthy of privileges and positions. A new belief system that many will embrace will facilitate willful compliance to the image and mark of the beast. A new privilege and reward system will be implemented. The ideology and wonders of the beast will reflect a form of popularly accepted sovereignty. It is not all about war and disaster. The worldwide conflict is also about truth in history and education. People will need a renewed mind operating through the Spirit under the influence of the Kingdom of God. The law of justice and reciprocity is exercised while the saints endure with patience and obedience (14:12).

In chapter 14 John sees a lamb with a 144,000 standing on Mount Zion with the Father's name on their foreheads (v. 1). The forehead is mentioned several times in Revelation. This might involve a sealing of the mind (reasoning, belief system) in regard to a particular persuasion and way of life. It also represents a kind of spiritual covering and salvific preservation for the redeemed servants of God (7:3).

The voices of heaven begin to sing as a great thunder a new song before the throne. No one could learn the song but the 144,000, who were virgins and persons without guile, without fault before God's throne. An angel flew in the heavens with the gospel of Christ encouraging the people of the earth to glorify and worship the Creator God.

Another angel makes a dramatic announcement: the great city of Babylon, which seduced the nations of the world with spiritual fornication, luxury, and corruption, has fallen (v. 8).

> And, behold, here cometh a chariot of men, with a couple of horsemen. And he answered and said, Babylon is fallen, is fallen; and all the graven images of her gods he hath broken unto the ground. (Isaiah 21:9)

> Babylon hath been a golden cup in the LORD's hand, that made all the earth drunken: the nations have drunken of her wine; therefore the nations are mad. Babylon is suddenly fallen and destroyed: howl for her; take balm for her pain, if so be she may be healed. We would have healed Babylon, but she is not healed: forsake her, and let us go every one into his own country: for her judgment reacheth unto heaven, and is lifted up even to the skies. (Jeremiah 51:7–9)

This announcement is important, because the third angel announces that anyone who received the mark of the beast, who empowered wicked Babylon, will be tormented (Revelation 14:9). There will be no rest for the unbeliever and the unrepentant. In contrast, the saints excel in faith and patience as they obey God

(13:10; 14:12). Those who have died in Christ have rest and reward for their good deeds.

The chapter ends with one who is like the Son of man sitting upon a cloud with a golden crown and sharp sickle in his hand (v. 15). An angel announces that the time is ripe to reap the harvest on earth. This is confirmed by two other angels coming out of the heavenly temple (sanctuary) of God. Outside the city will be flooded with blood. The unnamed city is understood by the followers of John to be Jerusalem.

The emphasis in chapter 15 is on the seven angels with the seven last plagues as a reflection of the wrath of God. John also shows those who have obtained victory over the beast, his mark, and his image. These saints begin to worship and sing the song of Moses. The temple of the tabernacle of heaven's testimony is opened for the seven angels to come out. One of the four living creatures presents the seven angels seven golden bowls of plagues, which will complete the process of the judgment of God. These bowls are to help win over people to the love and mercy of God. The same type of bowls (*phialas*) contained the prayers of the saints in Revelation 5:8, which came before God. Access to the temple is restricted until the administration of the plagues is completed. Prayer always has a major intercessory role in conflict.

Chapter 16 continues the theme of the fulfillment of the seven bowls. When the bowls are poured out, those who have the mark of the beast are critically affected. Those who worshiped the beast's image are more affected by polluted waters, the scorching sun, sicknesses, diseases, pain, sores, and ecological disorders. No parts or percentages of the earth are mentioned for these diverse conditions, unlike before. In Revelation 6:8 and 8:8–9, for example, select areas of the earth are designated for judgmental outpourings. The atmosphere is darkened and visibility is reduced. Some of these conditions may be continuous expressions of previous actions sent or permitted by God because of the lack of repentance among humankind. In fact, people get worse and blaspheme God because of their suffering ulcers and agony (v. 11). Their hearts again are hardened. But blessed are those who watch (guard) their lifestyle and behavior and avoid public shame.

There was an increase in the number and activity of evil spirits released out of the mouths of the dragon and his beast (v. 13). Greater manifestations of evil are unfolded in the vision. This means more false signs and more distorted, disordered personalities and psychotics are formed. More people will become defensive, depressed, disgusted, uptight, deceitful, possessive, and rebellious.

As conditions worsen, God again warns his people to be ready, for he comes suddenly as a thief (v. 15). Believers are told to watch and pray (Matthew 24:42; Revelation 3:3). Chapter 16 also refers to the preparation of the world for the battle of Armageddon. This is a subject unto itself. Many people today are anticipating and even desiring a world confrontation. But scholars say the exact space or location of the hill of Megiddo is not known. Zechariah 12:11 also mentions mourning over the valley of Megiddon.

What is certain is that Babylon leads the way in receiving the fierceness of God's wrath and anger. Other cities, some global cities of special importance, will also collapse and fall.

Chapter Seven

The Rise and Fall of Babylon the Great

In Chapter 17, one of the angels who had the seven bowls approaches John and invites him to come and see the woman of world significance. She is called a great harlot or whore. The woman as an empire excels in earthly splendor, seduction, and abominations. She sits at the waters of multinational populations. She has global reach and relevance. John was carried by the spirit into the wilderness. He was able to see this woman sitting upon a scarlet-colored beast with seven heads and ten horns. The woman was arrayed in purple and scarlet with gold, precious stones, and pearls. She held a gold cup filled with obscenities, which reflected her depraved condition. She was also drunk with the blood of the saints and witnesses of Jesus. On her forehead was written the name "Babylon," the great mother of harlots and abominations of the earth. Babylon was guilty of institutional imperialism and ruthlessness.

The plan of the beast and Babylon is to constantly engage the populations of the world as a form of preemptive control. The aim is to homogenize people and their way of thinking to facilitate surrender to the beastly mind-set. The beast uses schemes, symbols, language, education, ritual participation, public relations, public "rational" discourse, and a collective faith culture to achieve empire consensus. A collective faith culture is the mobilization of all forms of communication to reinforce certain beast beliefs about the beast, his administration, and ideology. Global society is "encouraged" to accept the teachings and self-deification of the beast. The repetition of this way of thinking eventually leads to a unique culture of faith.

This is reinforced by the reward power of the state and state religious apparatus.

The beast, which carried the woman, amazes those whose names were not written in the book of life. This is the beast that was and is not, but shall ascend from the bottomless pit into perdition, or destruction. John refers to seven kings who come and go (v. 10). The beast as a major participant is a force of evil persuasion and oneness with earthly rulers. Eventually the beast and his allies shall make war with the Lamb and lose the war. The Lamb, as King of Kings and Lord of Lords, is too powerful for the beast. But in the meantime, an earthly strategy and beastly unity or coalition is maintained. One allegiance, mind-set, and strength is shared by ten kings with the beast (v. 13). God moves so that they agree to act out his will by giving their kingdom to the beast until the final judgment of God arrives. These nations had no autonomy.

In the Old Testament, Babylon destroyed Jerusalem and led people captive. But in Revelation the power of the New Jerusalem, the city of God, replaces rival Babylon. The city becomes the ideal metropolis of God and humanity. In Revelation, symbolic Babylon is a combined type of Roman Empire on seven hills. Rome has almost complete worldly influence, corrupting power, and seductive attractions. Rome lures global citizens into her affluent arms (ways of life). Roman style, technology, military might, gems, wealth, and great pleasures are almost irresistible. This symbolic world of flashy imagination, dominance, and greatness appears deceivingly worthy to be worshiped and adored. Babylon and Rome represent a carnal mind-set, a perspective, and an acquired lifestyle. It is a perverted ideal, a defiled center of false glory and artificial peace. Its purpose is to create and maintain its own value system in opposition to God. The image of Babylon not only includes a city-nation global system but groups, institutions, and social, economic, and political structures. These groups are governments with ideologies, policies, rules, and meaning-making power.

Yet, Babylon fell because she destroyed herself, just like Rome. Her self-destructive evil knew no boundaries. She was out of control. God worked so that conditions were put in place to manifest the inherent weakness of the worldly system. In the case of Babylon and the cities of the world, God caused their global infrastructure to collapse. The vast systems of the beastly network failed. The collapse of world systems can also be attributed to the fact that inherently bad/evil networks are flawed and will eventually fail. Revelation 16:19 tells us Babylon was broken into three parts. Nations fell. Participating kings and leaders turned on each other (17:16; 18:11). The strength of God and his judgment was fatal. Their aggression was turned inwardly.

> And the ten horns which thou sawest are ten kings, which have received no kingdom as yet; but receive power as kings one hour with the beast. These have one mind, and shall give their **power** and **strength** unto the beast. ... And the ten horns which thou sawest upon the beast, these shall hate the whore, and shall make her desolate and naked, and shall eat her flesh, and burn her with fire. For God hath put in their hearts to fulfill his will, and to agree, and give their kingdom unto the beast, until the words of God shall be fulfilled. (Revelation 17:12–13, 16–17)

They Gave Their Mind to the Beast—at a Cost

In order for nations or regional providences to maintain some of their power and significance, they must collaborate with the beast-dragon. In the process, the dynamics of technical, financial, political, and shared infrastructure begin to expand. The dragon is better able to exact his program of international trade, ideological dominance, and theological hegemony. They all come together to deepen global linkages and control. That does not mean that these combined systems will work perfectly, because there are inherent weaknesses in any system. The second benefit of this collaboration is to draw in all the major political and financial players of the world in some kind of common participation. This collaboration produces a different world reality. It is a high-scale operation that affects vast numbers of people. This creates a "mindfulness" where collective focus is absorbed into the thinking and persuasion of the beast. This is the cost.

The question arises for any period before or during the tribulation: will believers organize themselves to deal with the global infrastructure of the beast? There are several responses to the question. In order to accomplish a major unified response from the church or groups of believers, they will need to put doctrinal differences aside. This is not likely to happen. Also, any coming together of believers might resemble a one-world, one-church, one-religion movement that would increase suspicion and mistrust. In addition, some believers have personal, regional, and group interests that benefit them. For instance, their politics are more informed by their cultural-social interests than their faith. Even within Christian organizations with a given set of beliefs, there is often so much mistrust, power struggles, and envy that very little could happen to counter Antichrist activities in the world. Overwhelming circumstances do not necessarily increase spirituality and unity. Only the coming of Jesus Christ Himself and the working of the Holy Spirit will bring the righteousness and justice needed for a strong and victorious people of God.

The Effects of a Turbulent Environment

Aside from the misery and sensationalism of the catastrophic events of Revelation 6 and other chapters, there are several impacting consequences of living in a global environment. Even without a *"tribulation period"*, human agony and increasing marginalization would be present in the world. The degradation of the quality of human life will increase as time unfolds. There will be new levels or hierarchies of inequality and stringent criteria for acceptance by those in charge. Fewer persons will participate in global fiscal management and the decision-making process. The human ability to endure physical and mental suffering will be fully tested. Revelation asks the question who will be able to stand (endure) 6:15-17. The remainder of Revelation deals with the beastly violence of foul thinking and corrupt ideas as self-destruction. The leaves of greatness begin to wither without the force of other nations to pluck it up (Ezekiel 17:9).

One major impact of ongoing turbulence upon people is the psychological effects created by extreme conditions. Stress and bipolar disturbances, for example, result from the continuous pressure people must endure under social and political duress. Personal relationships will be damaged or destroyed because of an air of mistrust, suspicion, and conflict. People will be increasingly marginalized, self-conscious, and alienated from each other. This tension will affect family life. Conditions will help create more personality disorders. Resentment will grip those who must deal with the wider world and institutional life. Despite attempts by the rulers to promote a caring, "in your best interest" assurance, people will be shaken by the economic and political climate. There will be a great need to make false assurances by false prophets. People will need a sense of peace, security, and hope.

Maintaining spirituality and authentic community will be difficult under tough conditions of mistrust and self-survival. The concern for believers is: how shall we best live in the world together until the Lord does come? People will need a powerful love (*agape*) environment to maintain for themselves a state of rest and peacefulness. It is under these conditions that the love of God works best.

Mind, Faith, and Culture

The second significant effect of a turbulent society will involve the tendency of the new world order to globalize thinking and culture. Culture has always existed as a wide-reaching, embracing network or unifying structure with its own reality. Norms and customs influence or control the prevailing culture. Culture develops over a period of time as practices become the norm. Traditions and past customs become difficult to change. However, new ideas and concepts do emerge that challenge old ways of doing things. The "Women's rights" movement, for example, has changed how contemporary society thinks and treats women. The media and technology has changed how people are able to view and transact global business. Constant messages, images, fads, educational curricula, and public communications serve to help to standardize a certain way of thinking and acting.

The beast or ruling agents of the world will generate uniformed global religious beliefs (syncretism) blended from generalized ideas from the major religions. It will be done in such a way that many people will gladly accept and respect the blended, "renewed" religious order. "Believing" persons will be favored in the distribution and eligibility of goods, services, and positions. Those closer to the dominant culture usually have greater access to social assets. People will receive education that is highly valued laden (loaded) with ideology, and restricted. Education will be designed to reflect the thinking of the ruling political overseers. God states in Isaiah that his thoughts are not our thoughts. The background of this scripture is the chronic historic challenges that Israel had with syncretism. There were gods of other nations present like Baal of Canaan. Elijah's challenge in 1 Kings 18:21 and Ephraim's involvement with the idols of Assyria in Hosea 14:8, were a part of foreign cultures and mind-sets. A part of the function of culture is shaping views, values, and public credibility. Singled-out persons or practices not compatible with the purpose of the beast are discredited by the beastly administration. Labels are placed upon those who do not seem to have "foreign views". This is a form of stigmatization and banishment. Labels are stamps of approval or disapproval.

Pierre Bourdieu, a French sociologist, advanced the notion of societal communications being assimilated into our consciousness. People will experience the "habitus" effect (habitual thinking), where conditioned ideas and opinions outside of the person become a part of collective social thinking. The social and believing mind-set of people is affected. Internalized views and understanding from the eternal world, along with social interactions, work to create a new human consciousness. People come to believe these are their own thoughts. They become decentered—they are made up of many competing ideas. The environment itself is full of misinformation and misleading ideas. Society exerts a seductive influence on the conscious life of the general public. Paths of "happiness" are mapped out through the entertaining activities of the world...this is that spirit of Anti-Christ (1 John 4:1,3). The false prophets reinforce ideologies that sustain the legitimacy of the beast.

> Beloved, believe not every spirit, but try the spirits whether they are of God: because many false prophets are gone out into the world. (1 John 4:1)

> And we know that we are of God, and the whole world lieth in wickedness. (1 John 5:19)

There are, it may be, so many kinds of voices in the world and none of them is without significance. (1 Corinthians 14:10)

> If we say that we have fellowship with him, and walk in darkness, we lie, and do not the truth. (1 John 1:6)

A "decentering" of personality results from a sense of being overwhelmed with so many things. A sense of selfhood becomes shaky. For example, it will be difficult to sustain an orderly mind and disposition when many messages, pressures, and demands are placed upon naïve hurting persons. Decentering leads to increased destabilization and acquiescence to normally unacceptable ideas. Some people will feel a sense of absolute lostness and disconnection. There will be a restriction of helpful information available to an insecure public. Faith will fade from the earth in many places. The beastly rulers will promote faith in themselves as "God" substitutes with honor and glory. The beasts demands that they be worshiped because they have the true healing "word." This is why the world needs an authentic view/perspective of real human life available to all through the Lamb. **"When the Son of man cometh, shall he find faith on the earth?"** (Luke 18:8). Not all persons have faith. (2 Thessalonians 3:2) And will he find a love community among believers? "A friend loveth at all times, and a brother is born for adversity" (Proverbs 17:17).

Shock Doctrine and Community

Another theme present in Revelation and in other eschatological scriptures is that of apostasy. Apostasy, or a falling away, reflects the mental and emotional state people will be in. People will buy into false logic and beliefs. They will live under conditions of overt or subtle intimidation and hegemony (the dominant ideas of society). Revelation 18:23 talks about the merchants of the world and their sorceries and deceptions. Society will distort ideas about life, collective justice, and inner security. Coping with identity in a shaken world will hinder the motivation for receiving truth and sound doctrine. It will be convenient to fall away or to embrace the prevailing ideas of the time. On the other hand, gospel acceptance will depend upon the strength and will of God's witnesses serving in an anointed ministry (Revelation 11:34). Much prayer will be needed to work in cooperation with the moving Spirit of the living God. A vague gospel without impact, spiritual depth, and manifestation will not reflect the power of a risen Christ (Hebrews 2:4). A church overwhelmed with issues, political alignments, or attachments to wealth, merchandise, and particular social groups will not be in position to minister to the masses.

Believers should personify spiritual influence in contrast to the centers of culture and generalized religion. There must be focus, love, and thoroughness in church outreach. The state of lukewarmness or neutrality can mean indecisiveness, wavering, and weakness, versus firm commitment. In fact, a love for God and his work should be unconditional. A weakly motivated church becomes an advantage for those who war against the church. They will encounter little resistance in their slander and distortions of truth.

The significance of collective life is prominent in scripture. In the Old Testament (Hebrew Bible), the term *people* (Am). In Greek "laos" is people. The Hebrew term "Am" means a group, a people, a nation of common ancestors, correlates to assembly and fellowship (*ekklesia* and *koinonia*) in the New Testament. These terms reinforce the importance of a called community of faith (Revelation 17:14).

The Kingdom versus Democratic Rule

In terms of a "free" society, the notion of democracy is also important. Democracy is the participation of the people in the decision-making process of government. Democracy in theory strives to create a just society for the general welfare of all—the greatest good for the greatest amount of people. But as we have seen in Greek history, the democratic process was seized by the ruling elite. Human democracy is replaced in the Bible with the theocratic Kingdom rule of our Lord. He calls it into existence and directs its righteous operation. However, people should not allow lukewarmness, complacency, laxity, and indifference to provide opportunity for deceptive others to seize the role of governance and control in society. The "rulers of the world" will almost eliminate the ability of the people to govern their own lives with clarity. Democracy is not theocracy. Democracy is not necessarily fair or universal. It tries to evolve under the circumstances. Some argue that democracy (like the Kingdom) seeks to create and maintain a universal sense of dignity. The difference is that secular dignity could include a sense of pride, excessive self-love (narcissism), and gross social inequality. Ecclesiastes declares that despite human achievements **"all is vanity and vexation".** In the book of Revelation those who endure look forward to the reign of Christ as the fulfillment of Davidic Rule. (Revelation 22:16, 21:5, 7)

It is therefore a challenge to create just, spiritual "voices" in secular society. Nevertheless, each believer should maintain a strong, credible witness in the "secular" world. Believers should watch all means of deception, shocking words, code words, false logic, and manufactured consent. "Status control" as a reward system is a part of social control. Rulers use the system to grant favor to some who are approved and impose restrictions on others. People become alienated from others through a false sense of loyalty and not truth.

> But there were false prophets also among the people, even as there shall be false teachers among you, who privily shall bring in damnable heresies, even denying the Lord that bought them, and bring upon themselves swift destruction. And many shall follow their pernicious ways; by reason of whom the way of truth shall be evil spoken of. And through covetousness shall they with feigned words make merchandise of you: whose judgment now of a long time lingereth not, and their damnation slumbereth not. (2 Peter 2:1–3)

> Likewise also these filthy dreamers defile the flesh, despise dominion, and speak evil of dignities. … To execute judgment upon all, and to convince all that are ungodly among them of all their ungodly deeds which they have ungodly committed, and of all their hard speeches which ungodly sinners have spoken against him. These are murmurers, complainers, walking after their own lusts; and their mouth speaketh great swelling words, having men's persons in admiration because of advantage. (Jude 8, 15–16)

Democracy on paper is a noble pursuit, but it is the real-life process that counts. A democratic structure may exist without a democratic process. During difficult times democracy can be dismissed. Naomi Klein puts forth in her book that during difficult times some may indulge in "shock doctrine," or politics that uses the occasion of fear and instability to introduce doctrines that work against the good of the people. During meltdowns and disasters, democracy is at risk (Exodus 5:10). People may yield to laws and practices that rob them of their actual freedoms. Under duress, people may welcome relief disguised as reform intervention. Under these conditions, intellectual and faith freedoms may be restricted. The standard for believers is the justice of God and the sanctity of life. Spiritual freedom creates a vibrant society. When justice is pre-empted the population may become vulnerable to distortions. Slanted laws and ideologies work for the benefit of a few at the expense of the many. This can de-energize or weaken the faith of a just people.

In the history of faith there has been conflict between the forces of church and state. This is why, for example, settlers came from Europe after the reformation to protect their sense of religious freedom. Martin Luther, John Calvin, and Huldrych Zwingli all had differences with the Pope and each other. The reformation affected governments and caused wars between Catholic and Protestant countries. African Americans claim that their faith helped them to overcome Jim Crow oppression. Modern Israel asserts that God protected them during the six day war. Many soldiers returning from the Vietnam War said that memorizing and repeating scripture enabled them to endure years of captivity and torture and return sane. Human crisis also increases the awareness that struggles exists on many fronts and levels. As we have outlined already, the spirit world of good and evil, the global world and the personal world of faith are in tension and conflict with each other. (Ephesians 6:12).

In the economic and industrial world there are great oligarchies (rule of the few) and tight linkages. Governments, secular institutions, labor, world markets, legislators, foreign alliances, technical systems, and supply chains are intertwined in one major operation. (Revelation 17–18). The individual citizen finds it difficult to be taken seriously when engaging such large connected bodies. Just pursuits can easily become overwhelmed with the reality of "negotiating" in a large, impersonal context. However, in the postmodern era of scrutiny and suspicion, opportunity is present with the "saints" to demonstrate the power of a Christ-centric faith. Authentic dealings in all relationships include avoiding seductive greed and lust for power. Genuine leadership leads people into the rightful access of an abundant life made available by and through God.

Under these conditions faith and prayer become indispensable. We must seek God in the face of universal systems. For matters of personal health, money management, friendships, sound thinking, family life, educational pursuits, and life strategies, we should seek divine help. Strong faith does not depend upon false allegiances of convenience but the leading of the Holy Spirit, which will always be at work in the world. The spirit carries on God's work.

Chapter 18 continues the discussion about the great Babylon and her downfall. A powerful angel descends from heaven who is filled with glory. The angel cries in a mighty way, with authority, and announces that Babylon has not only fallen but has been taken over by demons, every foul spirit, and hateful bird. Strange creatures (Isaiah 13:19–22; Jeremiah 51:37) inhabit the center place of idolatry and ultimate corruption. The one that had such great evil influence now becomes despised and deserted. The first is now last. Great Babylonian achievements within an advanced civilization now become a symbol of degradation and self-destruction.

John refers to the nations and merchants who have fornicated with Babylon. They drunk wine with her, lived in luxury, and brought her merchandise, and traded gold, silver, precious stones, pearls, fine linen, silk, high-grade wood (loved by the Romans for houses and fine buildings), ivory vessels, bronze, iron, and marble. Food, minerals, and farm products were not excluded: cinnamon, incense, ointments, frankincense, wine, oil, fine flour, wheat, cattle, sheep, and horses. Slaves and all kinds of clothes and goods were transported by ship in an elaborate worldwide operation. This empire utilized the services of fleets, sailors, and shipmasters. Great trade created great wealth, which creates great power and prestige. Trade and ingenuity made many ancient nations great. A false sense of security, military might, advanced human wisdom, and ideas lead to arrogance, more pride, and resistance to God. There was no need or will to negotiate with anyone. Babylon became addicted to pleasure, power, and undeserved praise. There was nothing left for her but double punishment for her deeds. This included plagues, torment, death, mourning, famine, and destruction by fire.

> Behold the day, behold, it is come: the morning is gone forth; the rod hath blossomed, pride hath budded. Violence is risen up into a rod of wickedness: none of them shall remain, nor of their multitude, nor of any of theirs: neither shall there be wailing for them. The time is come, the day draweth near: let not the buyer rejoice, nor the seller mourn: for wrath is upon all the multitude thereof. For the seller shall not return to that which is sold, although they were yet alive: for the vision is touching the whole multitude thereof, which shall not return; neither shall any strengthen himself in the iniquity of his life. They have blown the trumpet, even to make all ready; but none goeth to the battle: for my wrath is upon all the multitude thereof. The sword is without, and the pestilence and the famine which shall not return; neither shall any strengthen himself in the iniquity of his life. They have blown the trumpet, even to make all ready; but none goeth to the battle: for my wrath is upon all the multitude. The sword is without and pestilence and famine are within (Ezekiel 7:10–15).

John is also saying that Babylon restructured and reformulated collective human life through global trade and human interactions. Through globalization of trade and capital corrupting influences of new global values and politics came into existence. For example, in North Africa (AD 711 – 1450 and beyond) Islamic Arabs perpetuated slavery through trade, politics and force. Caravans carried gold from Nubia to Syria and Senegal banking centers for coinage. African female slaves were traded at twice the rate of Males who were sometimes castrated. Eunuchs were used as administrators, commercial agents, and harem guardians (Segal). Captives were used to advance Islamic causes. It became a corrupting influence on the world order. This movement occurs during a time when old national borders are fading. There is less allegiance to local identities and ways of life. New forms of social control emerge. The beast operates by creating a new culture and social controls. New technologies communicate a new collective mind-set and value system. The commodities of exchange in the world marketplace carry a new view of the world. Old ways and social distinctions are absorbed into the common culture of consumerism. People become partakers of the rational global belief system and institutionally led lifestyles. There is nothing just or holy about people complying with the indulgences of new world meaning, false logic, materialism, idolatry, and labor-assigned roles presented to them by the beast.

Babylon now experiences world rejection, loss of trade, and financial collapse. The voice from heaven cries out, "Come out of her, my people, that ye be not partakers" of her sins and plagues (Revelation 18:4). What does the angel mean when it refers to "partakers" of her sins? The word that is used in the Greek is *Synkoinoneo*. This contains the root word *Koinos* ("common"). It means to be a joint partaker, to mix one's self up in a thing, to get involved with, to be an accomplice, to actively sympathize with and cooperate with an activity. The voice from heaven encourages people to separate themselves. Flee from the influence of Babylon. Flee from the unclean city. Seek the holy city, Jerusalem. It is a city of truth, faith, and salvation. (Zechariah 8:3, 15-16).

The beast (global managers, social-political structures) oversees the credit system. The The beast influences what people are led to desire, with subliminal messages. Together with new forms of social and political life, they create centers of importance and involvement for people. That is globalization includes the establishment of global cities that specialize in a given commodity or expertise. For example, trade centers, stock exchange centers, manufacturing centers, educational centers where education becomes an export. I have visited cities that had many universities for many professions. One dean at a local university told me that the entire urban metropolis specialized in exporting education. Thousands of students came to that area from across the globe to study and then leave.

The tendency to "see more, want more, and get more" undermines sound family values and real cohesion. Technology and consumerism becomes a structure of power in themselves. To maintain this level of consumerism, the beast must communicate new images, ideology, and sense of satisfaction and reward. The beast appears to give, but in reality he drains the people dry in various ways. False prophets control communications and public relations. Ever-changing procedures help to regulate human life. The prophets make false promises that will not be fulfilled. People will still be needy and empty. The false promises make the beast look good because people want to believe the lie. They exaggerate the capacity and benevolence of the beast. (2 Thessalonians 2:11-12)

The chapter ends with the reassurance that Babylon will be thrown down with violence. Saints ought to rejoice. God is still working on behalf of his people, despite appearances. The beast that deceived, killed, and excelled in craftiness on a global scale will be lifted in disgraced and abandoned. For a while the beast was very successful. He had the power to finance his ambitions, communicate his ideas, manage his program, and use intimidating force. Beastly forces use the power of eminent domain to seize resources at will. But the power of faith and the power of God is what is used to finally overcome him and his seductive powers.

Chapter Eight

High on Joy: Worship, Marriage, and Victory

Chapter 19 opens with great rejoicing, "Alleluiah; Salvation, and glory, and honour, and power, unto the Lord our God" (v. 1). The people are happy. God's word is true, righteous, and just. He has with great justification judged the great harlot, who used her corrupting influence to abuse and kill the servants of God. Even the twenty-four elders and living creatures of heaven fell down and worshiped God as he sat upon his throne: "Praise our God ... Alleluia: for the Lord God Omnipotent reigneth" (vv. 5–6). The righteous could not contain themselves in this scene. Who could? David could not. Miriam could not. Joseph could not. Solomon could not. Esther and the Jews could not restrain themselves after they overcame the plot and schemes of Haman.

> And Mordecai went out from the presence of the king in royal apparel of blue and white, and with a great crown of gold, and with a garment of fine linen and purple: and the city of Shushan rejoiced and was glad. The Jews had light, and gladness, and joy, and honour. And in every province, and in every city, whithersoever the king's commandment and his decree came, the Jews had joy and gladness, a feast and a good day. And many of the people of the land became Jews; for the fear of the Jews fell upon them. (Esther 8:15–17)

> Let us be glad and rejoice, and give honour to him: for the marriage of the Lamb is come, and his wife hath made herself ready. And to her was granted that she should be

arrayed in fine linen, clean and white: for the fine linen is
the righteousness of saints. (Revelation 19:7–8)

Here we see the Lamb and his wife, the church, coming together
in heaven. The church is still made up of those who have been
called out (*ekklesia*). This is not necessarily the denomination or
institutional church. The marriage supper has been prepared. The
faithful church as believers together ought to be in a constant state
of preparedness (Matthew 24:44). Preparedeness is a New Testament
theme. It is seen in the parable of the ten virgins. Believers sought
to respond to God in faith and maintain a state of readiness, that
is be prepared for God in the call to death and accountability or
end time resurrection. 1 Thessalonians 4;13-18. John is told by
his escort to worship God. The true testimony of Jesus has come
forth through the spirit of prophesy. Blessed are they (the church)
who are called unto the marriage supper of the lamb (Matthew
25:5–10; Revelation 19:9). The church or ekklesia means those
who are called together, they are assembled together before Christ.
These passages connect the same ideas. They reflect the final
triumph of the armies and allies of heaven led by the King of Kings
and Lord of Lords. He defeats the beast, the false prophet, and their
follows. He is the warrior Messiah. The beast (Antichrist) and the kings
of the earth (leaders as powerful elites) could not together overcome
the captain of our salvation with their armies. Whatever form this
final warfare will take is not known. There is much speculation. But
the outcome is known. It is victory.

The Culmination

Although there has always been evil and injustice in the world, at
times it looked as if there would be no end in sight. This is far from
the truth. Those who walk by faith and upon every word coming
from God receives the light of Revelation, which assures us that the
brash, tyrannical forces of this world will be put down and put out.
Chapter 20 reveals the arrest and captivity of the beast, false
prophets, and their allies, who were cast alive into the lake of fire. The
evil one was indicted but not arrested. Jesus witnessed his eviction
from heaven (Luke 10:18). The devil went around seeking those he

might destroy, as reported in 1 Peter 5:8 and Job 1:6. But now justice has caught up with him. Jesus came to destroy the works of the devil, according to 1 John 3:8, and now the devil himself is bound. The time sequence of his reappearance and arrest is not specified.

The heavenly angel that appears has the key of authority and power to take custody, to loose and to bind. He takes the great chain, subdues and binds the dragon (serpent, devil, Satan, the evil one, deceiver), who is hurled into the abyss. There is no doubt from this scene who has ultimate reign and supernatural control. The deceiving devil is cast into the bottomless pit, shut up and shut down for one thousand years.

The millennium, or thousand-year period, is open for examination. Several major roles and interpretations include the following:

A. Lay hold to and bound Satan for a thousand years, and then take him out forever.
B. Justify and venerate the witnesses who lost their lives for Christ or the Word of God and who did not worship the beast, who did not receive the mark of the beast, and who will reign with Christ (Kingdom age) for a thousand years;
C. After the first resurrection of the just, some will be "left behind" while others will remain and suffer with the world. Eventually, all the dead in Christ will rise and reign. All people will be judged (Romans 14:9–10; Matthew 25:30–32; Revelation 20:11–13).

> Then cometh the end, when he shall have delivered up the kingdom to God, even the Father; when he shall have put down all rule and all authority and power. (1 Corinthians 15:24)

Those who are raised first are called blessed and holy. This is called the premillennial coming of Christ (before the thousand-year reign).

> Blessed and holy is he that hath part in the first resurrection: on such the second death hath no power, but they shall be priests of God and of Christ, and shall reign with him a thousand years. (Revelation 20:6)

The Thousand-Year Reign of Christ:

A Fixed Millennium or Timeless Period?

Revelation 2, 5, 22:21, 20:2–7
Actual, Figurative, Symbolic Eschatology
The End of the Church Age or the Beginning of the Church Age?

The reign of Christ occupies a prominent place in Revelation. That is clear. What may not be clear is the exact duration of this period. Is it an actual number, symbolic, or a long, indefinite period of time? "One day is with the Lord as a thousand years, and a thousand years as one day" (2 Peter 3:8). The symbolic number is also mentioned in Psalm 90:4, 105:8, and 1 Chronicles 16:15.

There is also the matter of the limitations placed upon Satan and when they are put into effect. Some believers say they are now in effect; others say they will go into effect at the millennium inaugural and the reign of the saints and the new age. When Satan is loosed at the end of the millennium, it is for a very short time before his ultimate destruction (Revelation 20:3). Before (16:16) the millennial reign of Christ, symbolic nations called Gog and Magog (Ezekiel 38:2, Revelation 29:8) lead nations to battle against Israel.

In Revelation 20:8, Gog and Magog are seen as two leaders or nation(s) who were against all believers. The origin of Gog and Magog (Ezekiel 38:1–6) is uncertain. It is believed that they originated from Asia and Asia Minor. Their task was to create chaos as leader(s) of some type of coalition/confederate. Ezekiel reports that Gog of the land of Magog, who was the chief prince of Meshech and Tubal, recruited Persia, Kush (Ethiopia), and Put (Libya) as allies. Gomer and its hordes were also recruited. This makes the number of allies seven, a number that represented major players in the known ancient world. It also symbolizes a multinational force convened to attack Palestine. Gomer represents a lawless band, posses, and warlords. This band may be made up of segments of unbelieving nations, including religious radicals and militants. Today the Ethiopian group would include Somalia, Sudan, and Eritrea. The battle mentioned in Revelation 16:16, 20:8 may represent a symbolic world war without the entire world. The nations named above typify the kind of adversarial response that could happen. Angels having the key to the bottomless pit are assigned the task of inflicting punishment and death (9:2–3; 20:1–3). The angel with the key incarcerated Satan in the pit (abyss) for a thousand years. Not only did Satan deceive the nations, but he also drove many to utter despair and depression. Those who were "stars" or persons of influence sustained massive attacks and lived under constant duress.

The thousand-year reign is inaugurated for three possible reasons:

1. To establish a working model and living example of righteous rule (Proverbs 29:2, 26). There have been so many failures in human rule, regardless of the label or form this rule has taken. No human government exists without major flaws, inconsistencies, fraud, and failure. The reign of Christ recognizes a higher level of righteous rule and just administration. Its structure, intent, and practices are grounded in Kingdom vision. It embraces equity and diversity in a classless society that operates according to the will of God and gifted roles in believers. It will be a theocracy by mediated sub-rulers whose center is God. For a higher level of human-divine cohesion, a higher level of leadership is required.

2. The established norms will include divine ways and means. Since the "law" of *agape* (divine love) will permeate the community consciousness of the righteous, little need for secular laws will exist. The divine norms of Kingdom life will suffice. The world of unbelievers may be more interested in a secular, godless society, political rulers tend to engage in meaning-making policies and may work to destroy a sacred meaning of collective abundant life. The aim of kingdom life is to exercise mutual respect, equalitarian exchange, and assigned responsibility through endowed abilities, insight, and godly understanding. Meaning-making includes establishing a collective purpose, social direction and specifying conditions in which people function or work. Creating meanings is often the result of social conditions for example is the commercial system going to be competitive or cooperative in nature. Will individuals and groups become self-oriented or work enhance the interest of "the divine" kingdom? Should the new kingdom advocate "*ultimate*" values or relative, situational values?

3. Human creativity will expand without greed-driven motives and deceptive strategies. The new order of things will include new, higher ways of thinking and acting. More excellent forms of relationships and agreeableness will exist. There will be righteous submission among all who serve God. This will model the "fruitfulness" of a divine covenant community, which will move away from the preoccupation with evil and evildoers to the eternal tasks and purpose of the Almighty. It will focus upon divine bliss in a new setting: ongoing wholeness in the presence of God rather than resisting the devil as an object of consciousness and concern (existential painful reality). The condition of newness and restoration does not exist in secular society. Past conditions of distrust, tension, and exploitation will cease to be. The human predicament of faith and suffering, good and evil, joy and alienation will be resolved. There will be peace, grace, and divine delight.

> In the multitude of my thoughts within me thy comforts delight my soul. (Psalm 94:19)

> His lord said unto him, Well done, thou good and faithful servant: thou hast been faithful over a few things, I will make thee ruler over many things: enter thou into the joy of thy lord. (Matthew 25:21)

> Make a joyful noise unto God, all ye lands: Sing forth the honour of his name: make his praise glorious. Say unto God, How terrible art thou in thy works! through the greatness of thy power shall thine enemies submit themselves unto thee. All the earth shall worship thee, and shall sing unto thee; they shall sing to thy name. ... Come and see the works of God: he is terrible in his doing toward the children of men. ... He ruleth by his power for ever; his eyes behold the nations: let not the rebellious exalt themselves. (Psalm 66:1–5, 7).

The Day of the Lord and Not A Date: Perspectives

The phrases "day of the Lord", "that day," and the "day of Christ" occur in many parts of scripture (Joel 1:15; Isaiah 2:12; 13:6; Zephaniah 1:7; Matthew 7:22; Luke 21:34; Philippians 1:6; 1 Thessalonians 5:2; 2 Peter 3:10). The "day" is usually seen as the time of the *parousia*, the return of Christ, resurrection, judgment day, the day of visitation, the day of wrath or reward (2 Timothy 4:1). Some believe that this will include the day when saints are caught up (*raptio*, 1 Thessalonians 4:17). No one has yet to precisely set forth a well-documented timeline in connection with the day of the Lord, the acceptable day (Isaiah 58:5), the time of tribulation, the *parousia*, the resurrection, and judgment (Revelation 11:18). There are still questions about Noah being saved from the flood, or saved through (protection) the flood, during the flood. Noah is mentioned here because some believers would argue that 'the day" of the flood represents a type of divine intervention for those who are ready for God to come and take them up and out of a turbulent world. Those who are, of course, prepared enter into the ark of safety will do so. The others are "left behind" (Matthew 24:36-40). But Noah never left the site-event of the flood. Locating the coming day, tribulation, or Kingdom reign is elusive. Jesus said no one knows the day or hour when the Son of man shall come (Acts 1:6–7; Mark 13:32). The significance of "the day" seems to indicate a motif or trend in regards to some kind of relation and relevance to end-time events.

Our concern is with discerning circumstances and activity related to seasons of duress, extreme hardship, tribulation, turbulence, and the seduction of materialism. The ability to engage in materialism will depend upon the economic status of the consumers. Marginal existence will force people to do with less regardless of their wants. These events would be influenced by influential personalities. They are also called the lawless ones. The lawless one(s) include those who are insensible, non-responsive, or against universal human and environmental concerns and justice. They may even feel themselves to be above the law or create laws for their own benefit. (2 Thessalonians 2:8, the lawless one in Greek is anomos) as we have discussed. there might be significant increases in apostasy, institutional evil, social and individual stress, and loss of significant absolutes and firmly grounded beliefs. Jesus said the greatest law is the law and practice of love. It is not necessarily about rules, but revelations and redemption.

> "Master, which is the great commandment in the law? Jesus said unto him, Thou shalt love the Lord thy God with all thy heart, and with all thy soul, and with all thy mind. This is the first and great commandment. And the second is like unto it, Thou shalt love thy neighbour as thyself. On these two commandments hang all the law and the prophets." (Matthew 22:36-40).

The type and aims of human global leadership and governance is important for human life and well-being. Under these conditions, the power of the Christian witness in the world (Revelation 11:3) is far more important than questions about doctrine and personal views. We should act out our view of the world and God's divine perspective. "Let your light so shine before men, that they may see your good works, and glorify your Father, which is in heaven" (Matthew 5:16). You are the salt of the earth. You are the light of the world. You cannot be hidden if you shine.

The chart that follows summarizes the phases of the establishment of theocratic kingdom reign. The people are gathered after they have overcome opposition by faith (1 John 5:4-5). The world kingdoms then become subject to Christ. Finally the Godhead, trinity, and triumphant Christ are exalted. (Revelation 1:17-18).

Revelation Theology Emphasis

The Powerful Godhead - Doxology (Worship)
Godhead Trinity Creator
Everlasting Doxology—Logos
Reigning Royal Ruler
Intercession Resurrection Restoration
Life-Generating, Life-Saving, Life-Personified
Glorified, Justified, Finalized

"Lift up your heads, O ye gates; and be ye lift up, ye everlasting doors; and the King of glory shall come in. Who is this King of glory? The LORD strong and mighty, the LORD mighty in battle. Lift up your heads, O ye gates; even lift them up, ye everlasting doors; and the King of glory shall come in. Who is this King of glory? The LORD of hosts, he is the King of glory. (Psalm 24:7-10)

Ultimate Dominion

The kingdoms of this world are become the kingdoms of our Lord, and of his Christ; and he shall reign for ever and ever. (Revelation 11:15b)

"Then cometh the end, when he shall have delivered up the kingdom to God, even the Father; when he shall have put down all rule and all authority and power. But thanks be to God, which giveth us the victory through our Lord Jesus Christ. Therefore, my beloved brethren, be ye stedfast, unmoveable, always abounding in the work of the Lord, forasmuch as ye know that your labour is not in vain in the Lord." (1 Corinthians 15:24, 57-58)

People: Assembled - Ekklesia

Overcoming Togetherness
Collective Mind-Set, Thinking Doctrine, Belief System
Purpose Covenant Destiny
Endurance—Ultimate End—Overcoming
Groupness Community Agreement
(Worship Prayer and Praise)

He that overcometh shall inherit all things; and I will be his God, and he shall be my son. (Revelation 21:7)

"I Jesus have sent mine angel to testify unto you these things in the churches. I am the root and the offspring of David, and the bright and morning star. And the Spirit and the bride say, Come. And let him that heareth say, Come. And let him that is athirst come. And whosoever will, let him take the water of life freely. (Revelation 22:16-17)

Spiritual Symbols: Expressed Meaning Continued

Oneness of Enduring Believer

One (heis): moving towards reconciliation and oneness, divine consensus—mind and experience cannot be negated, reduced, separated **The Trinitarian** (three): God into Himself Unity harmony—God and people fully connected Behold the Tabernacle of God: "And he will dwell with them, and they shall be his people, and God himself shall be with them, and be their God." (Revelation 21:3) **The Lamb**: Benevolent, proactive, sacrificial agent whose purity (blood) is a weapon against evil and prepares believers for the age to come. Seven horns and eyes—complete in rule, strength, and omniscience.

Zion Renewed

Look upon Zion, the city of our solemnities: thine eyes shall see Jerusalem a quiet habitation, a tabernacle that shall not be taken down; not one of the stakes thereof shall ever be removed, neither shall any of the cords thereof be broken. But there the glorious LORD will be unto us a place of broad rivers and streams; wherein shall go no galley with oars, neither shall gallant ship pass thereby. For the LORD is our judge, the LORD is our lawgiver, the LORD is our king; he will save us. (Isaiah 33:20–22)

The Cross: The Power of Reconciliation and Realignment

Victorious Submission

The cross: redemptive suffering, reverse of the curse, the humble, warrior (power), agent of judgment, conqueror of global systems (affects political-social order) **The mark**: certified, approval, burnt stamp **The trumpet**: sound of official warning, movement, expectation, announcement, and calling **Seven**: (*hepta*) perfect, completion, abundant fulfillment, actualized, attainment of God's will **Foul birds**: Scavengers, polluted ideas, ravenous Infectious: wicked influence (Ecclesiastes 9:18; Revelation 18:2, 4) Babylon: the seductive city of doctrinal prostitution **The city**: New Jerusalem, peace, newness, life eternal **suffering cross to glorious crown.**

And all mine are thine, and thine are mine; and I am glorified in them. ... That they all may be one; as thou, Father, art in me, and I in thee. (John 17:10, 21)

And all things are of God, who hath reconciled us to himself by Jesus Christ, and hath given to us the ministry of reconciliation; To wit, that God was in Christ, reconciling the world unto himself, not imputing their trespasses unto them; and hath committed unto us the word of reconciliation. (2 Corinthians 5:18–19)

The cross is a testimony. The cross represents the love and justice of God in the midst of conflict. There can be pain and peace. All the weight of a powerful deliverance was carried by Jesus the Suffering Servant and sacrificial Lamb. The living Lord is one with God and humanity. There is no victory without overcoming consistent opposition. "Be of good cheer I have overcome the world..."

Choosing Between Competing Claims

Claims of the Beast Versus the Claims of the Great I Am

Beastly Claims: Worldly Ruler

And it was given unto him to make war with the saints, and to overcome them: and power was given him over all kindreds, and tongues, and nations. ... And he had power to give life unto the image of the beast, that the image of the beast should both speak, and cause that as many as would not worship the image of the beast should be killed. And he causeth all, both small and great, rich and poor, free and bond, to receive a mark in their right hand, or in their foreheads. (Revelation 13:7, 15–16)

1. Transcendence (emperor worship and awe)
2. Absolute universal authority, law and military enforcement
3. The source of legitimate ideas, doctrine, values, beliefs, and practices (definition-making)
4. The shape of human authentic world order, society (to shape culture and religion as social control)
5. The right to control the world monetary-economic system
6. The right to control the world communications system
7. The right to establish and replace all other kingdoms by any means possible (deception, coercion, false prophets, miracles, etc.)

Messianic Claims: The Great I Am

I am he that liveth, and was dead; and, behold, I am alive for evermore, Amen; and have the keys of hell and of death. (Revelation 1:18)

Now unto him that is able to keep you from falling, and to present you faultless before the presence of his glory with exceeding joy, To the only wise God our Saviour, be glory and majesty, dominion and power, both now and ever. Amen. (Jude 24–25)

1. The Good Shepherd (worldwide flock or spiritual order)
2. The light (wisdom, purpose, knowledge)
3. Truth (reality without distortion or spin)

> 4. Way (practices, unifying love, and means to the good life)
> 5. Door (access to all ultimate things, salvation)
> 6. True vine (life-giving and sustaining substance)
> 7. Resurrection and the life (overcoming power of renewal, restoration, liberation, elevation)

Finalization: Prophesy and Fulfillment

In Chapter 20 Satan's time of suppression has come and saints prepare for the millennial administration.

The post-millennial age begins after the thousand-year reign is over. This follows the church age, when saints will reign. The church age started after the earthly resurrection of Christ in the Gospels. The time of "the rapture" in regard to the tribulation is widely debated. The final events now include the general resurrection, judgment, and the final destruction of the devil, beast and false prophet.

Some scholars argue that the thousand-year period is symbolic, not literal. The saints may or may not rule on earth. It could be a heavenly rule or both. During this period the activity of the Antichrist forces will be subdued or restrained. According to some scholars, there may be an interim kingdom. Some hold that once the kingdom is realized during this period, it shall remain. The key point is the asserted sovereignty of Christ over the cosmos. This also means that the sovereign Christ has a special relationship with the faithful church. This church became his special witnesses on earth. They are appointed to occupy leadership roles during the period of his reign. At some point, Satan is loosed for a brief period during or after the church age, only to be put down forever. Before that happens, he will attempt to get everyone he can to rally against God (Revelation 19:19). Gog and Magog represent anti-God forces on the earth (Ezekiel 38:1–5). None of these efforts to defeat Christ, the Lamb, will succeed. They shall overcome (Revelation 17:14).

At the appointed time, all the dead shall stand before God to give an account of their lives, deeds, and allegiances (Revelation 20:12). All those who refused to receive the righteous God, repent, and honor him are raised up and judged. They are assigned to the second death of punishment.

In chapter 21, John sees a new heaven and a new earth together. The former earth, heaven, and sea had passed away. The New Jerusalem, the city of God, the city of truth and faith, comes down from God out of heaven. This heavenly global city contrasts with the world city called Babylon, the city of evil. One city is the city of deception. The other is a city of truth (Zechariah 8:3). This city comes down as a bride adorned for her husband. This is a reminder of the bride-wedding theme present in the New Testament concerning the church. The emphasis is also upon newness and nearness (Zechariah 2:10–12). God dwells in the midst.

The Messiah is anticipated in Zechariah's vision reflecting the time of the restoration of the people of God from Babylonian captivity. The word *truth* (*emeth*) is so vital for restoration because the old Jerusalem did not abide in truth , this is why it fell to Babylon. "Even the Spirit of truth; whom the world cannot receive, because it seeth him not, neither knoweth him: but ye know him; for he dwelleth with you, and shall be in you." (John 14:17) "Thus saith the LORD; I am returned unto Zion, and will dwell in the midst of Jerusalem: and Jerusalem shall be called a city of truth; and the mountain of the LORD of hosts the holy mountain. And I will bring them, and they shall dwell in the midst of Jerusalem: and they shall be my people, and I will be their God, in truth and in righteousness." (Zechariah 8:3, 8) . It did not properly represent God in the world, especially in faithfulness regarding his covenant with Abraham . In matters of social justice she was not the real model for a king's city, a city of spiritual reality. The plumb line of the Lord is the measure by which God judges the city (Revelation 3:9–11).

The lying beast, master of deception and false information, false prophecy, and false administration, had to distort history and its interpretation in order to sustain the status of the beast and his co-rulers, the false prophets. The beast had to convince people that he had legitimate rule, doctrine, and judgment. Remember, debate, reason, and argument was admired and widely practiced in the marketplaces of the ancient world (Acts 17:17–23).

God is a God of truth. His promises are dependent upon this (Jude 11, 16, 19; Matthew 24:4–5, 10–12, 24; 2 John 2–4; 3 John 3–4; Revelation 3:7; 15:1; 19:11; 22:6; 2 Thessalonians 2:9–12). Truth (*emeth*) is a valid measure of one's word and deed, sureness, and stability (Jeremiah 9:5; Proverbs 14:25). The curse of darkness has been removed (Revelation 22:3).

In the last two chapters of Revelation, God continues to say that he will be with his people. He will be and continue to be their God. He still reaches out to "whosoever will" (22:17). God rewards those who believe The Word and participate in his righteousness.

The Alpha and Omega stands in direct contrast to outside dogs, evildoers, and liars (22:13–14). God will comfort his people and make all things new. Be assured in this current world of misinformation, slander, and spin machines that God's words are true and faithful. No one will be allowed to rewrite the true history of salvation or the history of faith in this book. (22:18–19).

God will help us to overcome. Do not identify with unbelievers, the fearful, who shall have their own punishment. The Lamb's wife, the bride, will still be present in the great holy city of Jerusalem. This city has been specially prepared and fortified for the eternal dwelling place of the people of God. It has great walls, twelve gates, a strong foundation, and precious jewels that adorn her. God himself shall be in her midst as the temple and glorified light. The gates shall not be shut; the saved shall walk freely because their names are written in the Lamb's book of life. The new city, new heaven, and new earth are created to fully symbolize and execute the ultimate ideal of a creation that far surpasses the beauty and magnitude of the old. God can and does perform it! In other words, believers will live out a structured life as lively stones, not the chaotic lives experienced in the world (1 Peter 2:3–6).

The scene will be supreme. The environment will be paradise (Genesis 2:8–10). It will be completely new: trees, a pure river of water, biogenerated (organically grown) leaves for healing of the nations, and of course, no more curse. John again must fall down and worship God, not the angel who showed him things to come. John is encouraged to keep the book open to give people another chance to get righteous, wash their robes, receive a reward, and gain rights to the tree of life inside of the gates of the city (the domain of God).

Jesus sends his angel to testify in the churches (22:16). He is the root and offspring of David, the bright and morning star, the Alpha and Omega, the beginning, the end, and forever. All that he is will be brought before us. He declares, "Surely I come quickly" (v. 20).

Lessons to Be Learned, Preparations to Be Made

The churches in Asia Minor became too close to the Roman government and localized culture. They also became too caught up in their affluence (Revelation 3:17–18; Matthew 6:20–21). In addition, their will or ability to maintain the integrity of ministry, sound doctrine, and sound apologetics (defense of the faith to the outside world) was compromised.

Believers need to pray for governments and government officials because they make decisions that affect the lives of both believers and unbelievers. Believers are people of law and order. When the righteous are in authority people rejoice, but when the wicked rule the people mourn (Proverbs 29:2). People need just rule, but they need to monitor events and policies that affect them daily. Believers cannot be strongly aligned with any party, government, or institution that will in time weaken them (1 Samuel 8:10-21). Often allegiances to a political party is more cultural, class and social than it is biblically or spiritually based. People tend to be protective of their own personal interest and social identification. Many may have little commitment to the well-being of others.

Laws and governments historically and politically operate in another realm, no matter how benign they may be for a while. Their norms, methods, and governance are generally in opposition to Kingdom life and values (Ephesians 6:12; Revelation 13:4, 7, 12; Revelation 17:12–13). In the apocalypse, governments are used as tools of darkness to exercise control and oppression as the gods of this world. This is why people of God are called to become vigilant persons in society.

The church in Ephesus left its first love without a long-term obligation to be the witness of the *agape* community (Revelation 2:4). What made them decline in their commitment to Christ and each other? The faith community must maintain a strong sense of community and oneness. Division weakens witness, strength, and public legitimacy.

Several of the rebukes to the churches in Revelation 2–3 have to do with influences outside of the church itself. References to Jezebel, the synagogue of Satan, and the Laodiceans seems to suggest that among believers that there is a connected cultural mind that is linked to the thinking, beliefs, and practices of the Roman world. The churches' accommodation with the social, religious, and political environment (even if unintentionally) resulted in an inconsistent performance of divine deeds. The unbelieving world fails to see a firm faith to address the human problem of war, greed, and injustice. The active presence of manifested ministry for all of God's people should be as powerful in a drug environment, for instance, as it is in a pulpit. Credibility includes global concern for a global mission which moves beyond selective morality, political and economic interest.

> *None calleth for justice, nor any pleadeth for truth: they trust in vanity, and speak lies; they conceive mischief, and bring forth iniquity. ... And judgment is turned away backward, and justice standeth afar off: for truth is fallen in the street, and equity cannot enter. Yea, truth faileth; and he that departeth from evil maketh himself a prey: and the LORD saw it, and it displeased him that there was no judgment. (Isaiah 59:4, 14–15)*

> *For thus hath the Lord said unto me, Go, set a watchman, let him declare what he seeth. ... Son of man, I have made thee a watchman unto the house of Israel: therefore hear the word at my mouth, and give them warning from me. (Isaiah 21:6; Ezekiel 3:17)*

Let us prepare for that which is already and that which is to come. Let us be watchful of our own motives and sense the will of God in contemporary life. Let us partner with God and each other in a stronger manner rather than with the powers of the world. Credibility (believer's righteousness) is a necessary currency in the world, especially in Babylon, where everything is discredited. No one should underestimate the power of evil to appear as legitimate. No one should overlook the supreme power of an omnipotent, all-knowing God, who is over this world. By faith and prayer we have access to this power. Do not forget that the false prophet/wolf can appear as a sheep (Matthew 7:15) or credible leader. Through the spiritual intervention of the great messianic Lamb of God, the forces of evil will be contained and terminated. Here is where the faith and strength of discerning saints lie.

> *For thou hast been a strength to the poor, a strength to the needy in his distress, a refuge from the storm, a shadow from the heat, when the blast of the terrible ones is as a storm against the wall. Thou shalt bring down the noise of strangers, as the heat in a dry place; even the heat with the shadow of a cloud: the branch of the terrible ones shall be brought low. ... He will swallow up death in victory; and the Lord God will wipe away tears from off all faces; and the rebuke of his people shall he take away from off all the earth: for the Lord hath spoken it. And it shall be said in that day, Lo, this is our God; we have waited for him, and he will save us: this is the* LORD; *we have waited for him, we will be glad and rejoice in his salvation. (Isaiah 25:4–5; 8–9)*

The Significance of the Book

In the great finale, after all works have been done and all struggles are over, the book of life will be opened and they who have kept the words of God's book shall be rewarded. He is a rewarder of them who diligently seek him (Hebrews 11:6).

> Let them be blotted out of the book of the living, and not be written with the righteous. (Psalm 69:28)

> … and there shall be a time of trouble, such as never was since there was a nation even to that same time: and at that time thy people shall be delivered, every one that shall be found written in the book. (Daniel 12:1)

> … help those women which laboured with me in the gospel, with Clement also, and with other my fellowlabourers, whose names are in the book of life. (Philippians 4:3)

Those whose names are written in the book of life are believed to be saved believers who have trusted and have served God without reservation (Revelation 3:5; 13:8; 20:12). They refused to buy into the life of the world and the superficial attractions of the worldly culture and (beastly) power. Instead, they are invited to the eschatological banquet supper of the Lamb. They belong to the real church as corporate believers.

Those who have overcome and have walked by faith shall be endowed with special privileges and "may enter in through the gates into the city" (Revelation 22:14). They "shall sit down with Abraham, and Isaac, and Jacob, in the kingdom of heaven" (Matthew 8:11).

> And I say also unto thee, That thou art Peter, and upon this rock I will build my church; and the gates of hell shall not prevail against it. (Matthew 16:18)

> And Jesus said unto them, Verily I say unto you, That ye which have followed me, in the regeneration when the Son of man shall sit in the throne of his glory, ye also shall sit upon twelve thrones, judging the twelve tribes of Israel. And every one that hath forsaken houses, or brethren, or sisters, or father, or mother, or wife, or children, or lands, for my name's sake, shall receive an hundredfold, and shall inherit everlasting life. (Matthew 19:28–29)

The act of sitting and judging implies leadership roles. It means that believers who have already championed the cause of Christ and demonstrated leadership capabilities will come to operate on a higher level in the Kingdom. End-times leadership requires those who are devoted, alert, and firm but compassionate, resourceful problem solvers and mediators. They are well informed, consistent change agents who act quickly when necessary after gaining revelatory insights. These persons never stop growing, learning, and preparing for *Sitz im Leben*, or situations in life. They walk carefully in the world to avoid unnecessary errors, misjudgments, and evil reprisals. They avoid unprofitable relationships and works that have no divine purpose.

> And have no fellowship with the unfruitful works of darkness, but rather reprove them. ... Wherefore he

> saith, Awake thou that sleepest, and arise from the dead, and Christ shall give thee light. See then that ye walk circumspectly, not as fools, but as wise, Redeeming the time, because the days are evil. Wherefore be ye not unwise, but understanding what the will of the Lord is. (Ephesians 5:11, 14–17)

They are not status seekers or headline grabbers, but minister unassumingly to accomplish the will of God. They operate with clear intentions and trustworthiness.

> But ye, beloved, building up yourselves on your most holy faith, praying in the Holy Ghost, Keep yourselves in the love of God, looking for the mercy of our Lord Jesus Christ unto eternal life. ... Now unto him that is able to keep you from falling, and to present you faultless before the presence of his glory with exceeding joy, To the only wise God our Saviour, be glory and majesty, dominion and power, both now and ever. Amen. (Jude 20–21, 24–25)

> He which testifieth these things saith, Surely I come quickly. Amen. Even so, come, Lord Jesus. The grace of our Lord Jesus Christ be with you all. Amen. (Revelation 22:20–21)

Summary: A Clearer Focus on Struggle or Strategy

The book of Revelation makes use of much symbolism, diverse images in the apparent struggle between the forces of good and evil. Yet, there is much that can be seen and understood from this cryptic message. The book occurs in the background of empires, mega structures and environmental upheavals. It deals with matters of suffering and pain, disease and health, but also faith and victory. The writer reports I know your works and faith...here is the patience and faith of the saints...Revelation 2:19, 13:10. Now the reader must decide what should be emphasized and applied for the task of overcoming the challenges of the future. New Testament scriptures encourage the leaders and followers of the faith to:

- Feed the flock of God who are among you (maintain your spirituality, develop critical thinking ability and perfect your teaching gifts.) The flock is God's connected community.
- Be sober, be vigilant, resist the evil one, your adversary Don't be complacent about the global picture and hardship. Watch as well as pray, develop a plan for self and collective management and discipline.
- Build yourself up in your most holy faith, have a high faith level. The just shall live by faith. Submit yourselves therefore to God, resist the devil and he will flee from you. Increase your in depth knowledge of important things. Ignorance will dismantle your ability to manage your life and thrive. End-time living requires excellent management skills, group edification, cooperation and accountability.
- Be careful to maintain good works. Be motivated to move beyond personal and cultural interest to a more comprehensive, ministry for the benefit of many. Seek to engage in deeds of love, Ministry without love is not ministry. All gifts work through love. We tell people "God loves you", but can they see it? All works that are of God manifest the glory of God by the spirit of God. There is a presence of God that is persuasive in every authentic ministry and witness.
- Be complete (the whole armor of God) in Him. Do not neglect the development of your mind and personality. There are many in this world who suffer from anxieties, emotional instability personality disorders and distorted, divisive relationships. If it is possible, live peaceably with all persons. Develop your ability to hear and respond to what the spirit is saying to you as you live with others. The god of this world is a wise master communicator. Discernment is critical for every believer. Learn to communicate not just talk.
- Be assured that the chief shepherd (of the sheep) shall appear. He is a rewarder of those that diligently seek Him. Revelation demonstrates that God has not abandoned His creation. Look not at the things that are seen, but the things that cannot be seen with the natural eye. The love of God within the family of faith is a light that will not be hidden.

- Develop an economic plan for fiscal stability and responsibility as good stewards of Jesus Christ. You are accountable to him in the management of your resources and gifts. Avoid being seduced into poverty or extravagance. Do not abuse the oil and the wine. (Revelation 6:6) Discover God's system and divine economy. Manage your affairs with prayer, care and caution. God can and will multiply your resources beyond the level of your comprehension.

These are just a few points of emphasis that can be expanded to design a more complete strategy for living within the principalities and powers of this world now. Live with a kingdom mind-set and sense of a divine perspective. Lord show us the way. (John 14:5)

> That the God of our Lord Jesus Christ, the Father of glory, may give unto you the spirit of wisdom and revelation in the knowledge of him: The eyes of your understanding being enlightened; that ye may know what is the hope of his calling, and what the riches of the glory of his inheritance in the saints, And what is the exceeding greatness of his power to usward who believe, according to the working of his mighty power, which he wrought in Christ, when he raised him from the dead, and set him at his own right hand in the heavenly places, Far above all principality, and power, and might, and dominion, and every name that is named, not only in this world, but also in that which is to come. (Ephesians 1:17-21; 5:14)

> The famous chemist Percy Julian once told his impatient, tired trusted partners during adverse times: **Sleeping may be dangerous to your health**. **(Rise for the Prize).**

> When **"the end"** of this life-world does arrive as we know it, Christ will reign. The kingdom will be put under the full authority of God. All those who were faithful and steadfast will see the rewards of their labor. (1 Corinthians 15:24-25; 57-58)

The Lordship of Christ, I am Alpha and Omega and dominion. I am alive forever more. God has made us an army and kingdom of intercessors, priests, and prophet, faithful witnesses forever and forever. Blessed is He that sits upon the throne and unto the Lamb who is worthy of his glory. **Amen**

Select Bibliography

Agnese, Giorgio. *Ancient Egypt*. New York: Barnes and Noble Publications, 2006.

Aune, David. *Word Biblical Commentary: Revelation, Vol. A, B, C*. Dallas: Word Books, 1997.

Bourdieu, Pierre. *Outline of a Theory of Practice*. Cambridge: Cambridge University Press, 1977.

Bracher, Robert G. & Hatton, Howard A. *The Revelation to John*. New York: Unified Bible Society, 1993.

Cook, Stephen. *The Apocalyptic Literature*. Nashville: Abingdon Press, 2003.

Conzelmann, Hans. *Acts of the Apostles: A Commentary*. Philadelphia, Fortress Press 1987.Daniels, Patricia & Hyslop, Steve. *Almanac of World History*. Washington, D.C.: National Geographic Society, 2003.

Ehret, Christopher. *The Civilizations of Africa: A History to 1800*. Charlottesville: University of Virginia Press, 2002.

Felder, Cain. *Troubling Biblical Waters: Race, Class, and Family*. Mary Knoll, N. Y.: Orbis Books, 1989.

Fiorenza, Elisabeth. *The Book of Revelation: Justice and Judgment*. Minneapolis: Fortress Press, 1998.

Ford, J. Massyngberde. *Revelation*. Garden City, N.Y.:: Doubleday, 1975.

Garrett, Laurie. *The Coming Plague: Newly Emerging Diseases In A World Out Of Balance*. New York Penguin Books 1995.

Hartman, Louis F. & Di Lella, Alexander A. *The Book of Daniel*. Garden City, N.Y.: Doubleday, 1976.

Henze, Paul. *Layers of Time: A History of Ethiopia*. New York: Palgrave Macmillan, 2001.

Hoogvelt, Ankie. *Globalization and the Postcolonial World: The New Political Economy of Development*. Baltimore: Johns Hopkins University Press, 2001.

Klein, Naomi. *The Shock Doctrine: The Rise of Disaster Capitalism*. New York: Picador, 2007.

Leary, Mark & Kowalski, Robin. *Social Anxiety*. New York: The Guilford Press, 1995.

Long Jr., Edward. *A Survey of Recent Christian Ethics*. New York: Oxford University Press, 1982.

Morris, Leon. *Revelation*. Revised Edition Grand Rapids, Mich.: Eerdmans Publishing, 1987.

Mounce, Robert. *The Book of Revelation*, revised ed. Grand Rapids, Mich.: Eerdmans Publishing, 1998.

Oppenhein, A. Assyrian and Babylonian Historical Texts (including Ethiopian Reference) In The Ancient Near East Volume 1. James B. Pritchard editor. Princeton: University Press, 1958.

Peter-Contesse, Rene & Ellington, John. *A Handbook on the Book of Daniel*. New York: United Bible Societies, 1993.

Roloff, Jurgen. *Revelation*. Minneapolis: Fortress Press, 1993.

Segal, Ronald. Islams Black Slaves. New York: Farrar, Straus and Giroux, 2001.

Shillington, Kevin. *History of Africa*. Second Edition. New York: Palgrave Macmillan, 2005.

Tilly, Charles. *Democracy*. Cambridge: Cambridge University Press, 2007.

Yamauchi, Edwin. Africa and the Bible. Grand Rapids, Mich.: Baker Academic, 2004.

Index

Index